DAILY READ

FROM

WILLIAM TEMPLE

COMPILED BY

HUGH C. WARNER

Vicar of Epsom

MOWBRAY
LONDON & OXFORD

This paperback edition published 1981
by A. R. Mowbray & Co. Ltd
Saint Thomas House, Becket Street,
Oxford, OX1 1SJ

ISBN 0 264 66804 9

Copyright © Hodder & Stoughton, 1948

First published in 1948
by Hodder & Stoughton,
this edition is reproduced from the original text
set by The Camelot Press Ltd, and is
printed in Great Britain by The Thetford Press Ltd.

FOREWORD

ALL good things wear well. History can be cruel in its selectivity, rapidly discarding what is in vogue in any one generation and only retaining for subsequent generations what is of lasting significance.

It is perhaps all the more noteworthy therefore that both the personal influence as well as the substantial writings of Archbishop William Temple are still conspicuously in vogue. It is almost tantalising for someone from another generation who did not actually know this great Archbishop to find that his influence is so clearly lasting. Perhaps that has something to say about the unfading quality of saintliness. Furthermore you have only to read a small amount of William Temple to know that you are engaging with a master of the English language and with a scholar whose sublime gift was his ability to express the most profound reflections in language which is deceptively simple and memorably clear.

But perhaps there is a further reason why the re-issue of this book of Daily Readings is timely and indeed already overdue some thirty years after it was first published. The years since the death of Archbishop Temple have seen an unhealthy swing in theology and spirituality. The day of an over-emphasised social gospel and the demand for relevant concern has given way to what could be in danger of becoming an age of enthusiastic pietism, engaged only with personal spirituality and a simplistic apologetic for Christian truth. In the writings of William Temple there is a refusal to prise the one whole gospel into two parts. For William Temple there were not two rival gospels – the gospel, and the social gospel. For him as a christian apologist of outstanding merit there was in fact only one whole gospel with its roots reaching deeply into a scriptural and traditional spirituality and its branches stretching out into the surrounding environment of the contemporary world and all its concerns. If for no other reason we should welcome this re-issue of the writings and sayings of a man whom time increasingly proves to be at one and the same time both scholar as well as saint, and prophet as well as priest and pastor.

+ MICHAEL MARSHALL
Bishop of Woolwich

June 1981

COMPILER'S FOREWORD TO FIRST EDITION

MORE than most people of his day, Archbishop Temple had the gift of expressing in a sentence or two the most profound conceptions of religion and philosophy. To hear him speak was always an intellectual joy; the turn of his sentences, their cadence, and the amazing way the chain of thought resolved itself in a single complex whole with never a word out of place, or the slightest hesitation in delivery—this is unforgettable. While listening, one wished to live with the thoughts he created, to taste them again at leisure, drawing upon the wealth of experience and wide reading that lay behind all he spoke and wrote.

This anthology will, I hope, serve to answer this need. Five years as his personal chaplain brought one into very close contact with him, and that has been a privilege for which this work is in some little way a thank-offering.

An index to references will be found at the end of the volume.

My thanks are due to the following for permission to reproduce from the late Archbishop's books: Mrs. Temple, and Messrs. Eyre and Spottiswoode, Ltd., Hamish Hamilton, Longmans, Macmillan and Co., Ltd., National Book Council, Student Christian Movement Press, Society for Promoting Christian Knowledge. Above all, I must thank Miss Jeal for her untiring labour typing and re-typing the whole of this script.

HUGH C. WARNER.

CONTENTS

DAILY READINGS
FROM
WILLIAM TEMPLE

JANUARY

January First

1. CREATOR GOD

The essence of the doctrine of Creation is not that God inaugurated the existence of the world at a particular moment of time, but that the world owes its existence—not only its beginning—to His volitional activity.

2. GOD'S CONTINUING ACTION

It is not that there is a fixed natural order laid down once for all by God, and since left alone, with which from time to time He interferes; it is that all the while He is acting, only all the while it is appropriate, on most occasions, to follow a regular course, as does the ordinary man of regular habit in the conduct of his daily life.

3. IMMANENCE OF GOD

Divine immanence is always and only the activity of a transcendent Personality, and operates, after the manner of personal action, by infinitely various adjustments which exhibit constancy of character in face of varied situations.

January Second

4. CHRIST: FACT NOT INFERENCE

Always remember that Jesus Christ is offered to men first and foremost, not as a problem but as a solution. . . . We do not start with the life recorded in the Gospels and ask, "What are you going to say about it? Is it not really so marvellous that you are bound to call Him Divine?" But . . . we shall say instead, "The world is governed somehow; there is a rational principle at work in it; and the character of that principle is seen in Jesus Christ."

5. KINGSHIP OF CHRIST

While we deliberate, He reigns; when we decide wisely, He reigns; when we decide foolishly, He reigns; when we serve Him in humble loyalty, He reigns; when we serve Him self-assertively, He reigns; when we rebel and seek to withhold our service, He reigns—the Alpha and the Omega, which is, and which was, and which is to come, the Almighty.

6. COMPANIONSHIP WITH CHRIST

There is the secret of finding the Holy Spirit in life; it is the companionship with Christ, constant and perpetual, in worship, in all the daily tasks of life as we try perpetually to refer to Him our aspirations and ambitions, and by His mind to check all our thoughts, feelings and desires, and in the service of the kingdom which He came to found, and for which He calls on us to be His fellow-workers in preparing.

January Third

7. THE HOLY SPIRIT

Holy Spirit is God's answer from the depths of our being to the call which He gives from His highest Heaven.

8. LOVE IS HOLY SPIRIT

All the great theologians have always said that the love wherewith a man loves God or his neighbour is the Holy Ghost. It is not the *work* of the Holy Ghost only, it *is* the universal spirit at work in the hearts of His creatures.

9. THE ELECT

The elect are those to whom, through no merit of their own, great opportunities of influence or service have come. The greatest of all the opportunities there is, or ever can be, in the world is to know the character of God, the ultimate reality upon whose Will everything depends; and so to know it that our hearts are called out in sympathy so that we not only do His Will thinking it must be sensible to do what He wants, but that we want to do it. That will to do it, in the heart of man, that is the *Holy Spirit*.

10. THE CHURCH

When His visible Presence was withdrawn from men's sight, what was left as the fruit of His Ministry? Not a formulated creed, not a body of writings in which a new philosophy of life was expounded, but a group of men and women.

11. OUR DEBT TO THE CHURCH

If it seems to you that the Church as organised has somehow lost sense of proportion, remember that only through the Church has the Gospel ever reached you, and that only through the Church can it reach the ages far ahead. And you will do more service to the cause of Christ by bringing in what reality you can into its life than you can ever render by staying outside and doing what seems possible to you, or you and your few friends, in isolation.

12. "A PRESSURE-GROUP"

When Dr. Oldham issued a questionnaire on the Nature of the Church, one American professor opened his reply with the words: "It is evident that the Church is a pressure-group." I know no phrase which it would be harder to interpolate harmoniously into the Epistle to the Ephesians.

January Fifth

13. WORSHIP DEFINED

To worship is to quicken the conscience by the holiness of God, to feed the mind with the truth of God, to purge the imagination by the beauty of God, to open the heart to the love of God, to devote the will to the purpose of God. All this is gathered up in that emotion which most cleanses us from selfishness because it is the most selfless of all emotions—adoration.

14. WORSHIP AND SOCIETY

The heart of moral improvement, the heart of moral progress, therefore also of social progress, and the amelioration of this world's bitter condition, is always to be found in worship, worship which is the opening of the heart to the love of God and the exposure of the conscience to be quickened by it.

15. LANGUAGE IN PUBLIC WORSHIP

For public worship the language should be the most beautiful we can find for the purpose, suggesting in its beauty the reverence we owe to the Divine Majesty. Moreover, it should very often express not only the things we do feel, but the things we ought to feel, so that we may, by our prayer, teach ourselves to feel those things more thoroughly than we have done.

January Sixth

16. SUGGESTION FOR PETITIONARY PRAYER

He knows what we want before we ask it. Then why ask? Why, because there may be blessings which only are effectively blessings to those who are in the right condition of mind; just as there is wholesome food which is actually wholesome only to those who are healthy in body. If you give the best beef to somebody in typhoid fever, you do him great harm. The worst of all diseases of the soul is forgetfulness of God; and if everything that we need came to us while we forgot God, we should only be confirmed in our forgetfulness of Him, in our sense of independence of Him. . . . Over and over again, it will happen that, whether or not God can give the blessing which, in His love, He desires to give, will depend on whether or not we recognise the source from which it comes. The way to recognise that He is the source of the blessings, and that we need them, is to ask.

17. PRAYER—ANSWERED AND UNANSWERED

What is very startling . . . is the abundance of testimony given by those who have had intimate experience of men's spiritual life to the conviction that in the early stages prayer receives literal fulfilment with great frequency; that later on this becomes less frequent, until it seems almost to cease, as though God at first gives encouragement of the most obvious kind and later withdraws this in order to evoke a deeper trust.

18. ESSENCE OF PRAYER

The proper outline of a Christian prayer is not "Please do for me what I want." It is "Please do with me what You want." That prayer will always be answered in proportion to its sincerity.

19. OBJECTIVITY OF THE SACRAMENT

When faith exists as a struggle to believe in spite of empirical and temperamental pressure to unbelief, when the whole life of feeling is dead, when nothing is left but stark loyalty to God as He is dimly and waveringly apprehended to be—then the sheer objectivity, even the express materialism, of a sacrament gives it a value that nothing else can have.

20. SACRAMENTAL PRESENCE IN EUCHARIST

It is in the context of the sacrifice of Christ, spiritually accomplished in the Upper Room, historically consummated on the Cross, and representatively offered on our altars to-day, that we must consider the question of the Sacramental Presence of Christ in the Eucharist.

21. SACRAMENTS AND MAGIC

If it be held that episcopal ordination confers a power of making sacraments, so that when an episcopally ordained priest celebrates the Eucharist something happens in the world of fact which does not happen on any other condition, then these bodies have no real Sacraments. But that is a theory to which I find myself unable to attach any intelligible meaning. It is admitted that the peril to which strong sacramental doctrine is most liable is that of falling into conceptions properly described as magical; and this theory seems to me to lie on the wrong side of the dividing line.

January Eighth

22. THE OLD TESTAMENT

What we find in the Old Testament Scriptures is not mainly, if at all, authoritative declarations of theological doctrine, but living apprehension of a living process wherein those whose minds are enlightened by divine communion can discern in part the purposive activity of God.

23. OLD TESTAMENT ECONOMICS

The economic legislation of the Old Testament . . . is precisely the allowing of free play to individual initiative in such a way that no man acquires the right to possess, to exploit or to hold down his neighbour.

24. Loss of Revelation

On the Biblical view the *locus*, the sphere, the area, of revelation, is primarily the historic event, not thoughts in men's minds at all, but the thing that happens—the deliverance from Egypt, the retreat of Sennacherib, the Exile, and the Return. In these things we are to read the action of God, His purpose, His judgment.

January Ninth

25. Psychology and Knowledge

If a psychologist assures me that I believe in God because of the way in which my nurse used to treat me, I must retort that he only holds that belief concerning my belief because of the way in which his nurse used to treat him.

26. The Principle of Explanation

Whenever you trace any event or observed fact to the action of intelligent purpose you have explained it; if you understand the purpose and sympathise with the object you are satisfied. So far as I am aware, there is no other principle in our experience about which this is true.

27. Man's Convenience and the Course of Nature

It is good for a man to know that the course of nature is not devised for his convenience; for his benefit indeed it is devised— for it is to his benefit that his individual convenience should not be considered.

January Tenth

28. Beauty

When you listen to beautiful music, where is the beauty? You do not create it: you do not invent it—you find it. And yet you will not find it unless you have the understanding of music which qualifies you to be sensitive to it. It is the same with beauty everywhere. . . . And so in the Holy Communion Christ offers Himself in all His fullness of holiness and love to be ours, but whether you receive Him depends on the insight of your faith, on how far you are conscious of your need of Him, on how far you are sincere in seeking to be united with Him in His offering of Himself to the Father.

29. Good in Beauty

I can see no good in Beauty which no one at all perceives—neither man nor angel nor God. A beautiful object is only a potentiality of good until it is perceived and appreciated. But when it is appreciated, the percipient mind finds the good in the object; it *enjoys* the apprehension, but it *admires* the work of art or of nature.

30. Beauty

There is more in Beauty than Beauty alone. There is communication from, and communion with, personal Spirit.

January Eleventh

31. Obligation Towards Truth

Willingly to believe what is suspected to be false is felt to be an offence against the order of reality. This feeling is quite unreasonable if the order of reality is a brute fact and nothing else; it is only justifiable if the order of reality is the expression of a personal mind, for the sense of moral obligation towards Truth is of that quality which is only appropriate in connection with personal claims.

32. Agnostics

This quality of reverence for Truth is specially evident among those who have felt bound, out of loyalty to Truth itself as they had been able to receive it, to abandon the belief which alone could justify it. It would seem as if there were some potent force compelling in them an attitude of mind which their own convictions have rendered obsolete. All this is intelligible on a basis of avowed Theism, but highly paradoxical on any other.

33. Limitations of Explanation

If the scientist were asked to explain why he must give loyalty to Truth precedence over all other considerations, he would find it hard to comply. It does not seem to him unreasonable, but he cannot give a reason for it, because it is the rational presupposition of all particular "reasons."

34. GOOD AND RIGHT

Right is the Good as presented to mind practical; Good (as applied to an act) is Right as presented to mind contemplative.

35. ABSOLUTE AND RELATIVE GOOD

What is in itself second best is best for certain persons or in certain circumstances. But then for them it *is* best. In applied ethics or moral theology the logical principle that "relative terms are in their relations absolute," has vital importance. "Big" is a relative term; but an elephant *is* big in relation to a mouse. True relativity never involves uncertainty.

36. CAUSATION BY APPARENT GOOD

So soon as there is an entity which has even once been determined in its conduct, not by the impulsion of efficient causation but by the lure of apparent good, a new principle, utterly incapable of reduction to efficient causation, has made its appearance, and any coherent account of the universe must allow for it. But to do this is at once to pass from a materialistic to a spiritual interpretation of the universe.

January Thirteenth

37. SOVEREIGN STATE

Internal tyranny and external aggression must alike be expected from States which are regarded by their subjects and their administrators as absolutely sovereign. Yet there is no logical ground for regarding the State in any other way except faith in God.

38. THE STATE AND CHRISTIAN PRINCIPLES

It can hardly be said that the Church ought to denounce the State every time the State acts on less than absolutely Christian principles; indeed the State has actually no right to act on those principles unless the whole body of citizens desires this.

39. THE STATE AND PROPERTY

The only way to escape the authority of the State is to own no property at all; and that would be a deprivation of means to do spiritual work such as it would be madness to incur unless the alternative were a compromise of fundamental principles.

January Fourteenth

40. OBJECT OF INDUSTRY

It is clear that, in the natural order of things, God's order, the object of all industry is the supply of men's wants; in the language of the economist, the consumer is the person whose interest should be supreme in determining the whole process; for his sake goods are produced; and finance comes in as the servant of production. But in our world, goods are produced, not primarily to satisfy the consumer, but to enrich the producer.

41. INDUSTRIAL SLAVERY

When we look at the industrial system that we have allowed to grow up it is surely quite apparent that at least in many parts of the world labourers are treated by the system, even if not so in the intention of those who work it, as only parts of the means of production. And it can never be right to treat human beings so.

42. FUNCTION OF INDUSTRY

Reformers sometimes demand that industry should become co-operation for public service instead of competition for private profit. That puts it wrong. Industry always is co-operation for public service, but we often treat it as if it were competition for private profit.

January Fifteenth

43. REVERENCE FOR SEX

The first necessity for a truly Christian philosophy of sex is to pass from the phase where sex is a matter of shame to that where it becomes an object of reverence. Through it God allows to men the incomparable privilege of co-operating with Him in the creation of His own sons and daughters, called to eternal fellowship with Him. How sacred a thing is this!

44. LIFELONG SEX UNION

If you put together the things said by our Lord and by St. Paul on this subject (sex), you will find the principle which holds them together is that this union should be, and is meant to be, an expression of a spiritual union so complete that it must be lifelong.

45. BROKEN MARRIAGES AND DIVORCE

I see no reason whatever to suppose that, contrary to His practice in all other connections, our Lord intended to legislate for His Church in this matter of marriage. What is best to be done when the ideal is once made impossible, He did not say. He did not blame Moses for making a concession to the hardness of men's hearts, and there is no reason to suppose that a like liberty is forbidden to us. But He did say that only because hearts were hard was any concession given.

January Sixteenth

46. ATHEISTIC EDUCATION

An education which is not religious is atheistic; there is no middle way. If you give to children an account of the world from which God is left out, you are teaching them to understand the world without reference to God. If He is then introduced, He is an excrescence. He becomes an appendix to His own creation . . .

47. A CHILD'S HOME

The most influential of all educational factors is the conversation in a child's home.

48. EDUCATION IS ASSIMILATION

The mind receives and assimilates its environment of truth, beauty and goodness, so that these become part of its own texture. To forward this is the task of "education"; that very word means "nourishment."

January Seventeenth

49. EUCHARISTIC PRESENCE

Christ is not locally present in the Sacrament; . . . and language which implies a local presence of Christ ought to be scrupulously avoided; there is such language in some popular books of Catholic devotion; a phrase like "The Prisoner of the Tabernacle" is quite indefensible.

50. Eucharist: Taking and Eating

That we should "take" and "eat" is an indispensable aid which the sincere Christian cannot omit; but the one thing that matters is that we should "feed upon him in our hearts."

51. Eucharist more than Fellowship

The Eucharist is not first and foremost a meal of fellowship. No doubt it was instituted in the midst of a meal of fellowship, but in itself it is something more and other than that.

January Eighteenth

52. Holy Baptism

By birth I came into the world as a child of my parents; by Baptism I was brought into the Church as a "member of Christ." My parents could care for me or neglect me; they could not prevent my being to all eternity their child. My fellow Churchmen could teach me or ignore me; they could not alter the fact of fellow membership.

53. Infant Baptism

One of the advantages—(there are disadvantages also!)—attached to the practice of infant Baptism is its clear expression of the truth that we do not make ourselves Christians. The fact that we are Christians is not due to any act on our part; it is due to the act of God in Christ through the Holy Spirit.

54. Lay Baptism

The Church recognises Lay Baptism, though of this Sacrament as of others the bishop is the proper minister, "or he to whom the bishop may entrust it"; he does this by the very act of ordaining a priest, and gives authority to a deacon to baptise "in the absence of the priest." It is hard to see any difference in principle in the case of the Eucharist.

January Nineteenth

55. Grace and Inertia

The only man who has experience of being shaped by divine grace is the man whose will is in fact surrendered and is become the energetic instrument of that grace; such a man can never suppose

15

that his proper reaction to the doctrine that all good is from God alone is to be found in inertia.

56. SIN AND ABOUNDING GRACE
Thus St. Paul was involved in great dialectical difficulties by those who said that his doctrine of grace led straight to the conclusion that we should continue in sin that grace may abound. So it does— for those who are not in Christ; but then the doctrine has no application to them at all; and those who are in Christ cannot continue in sin; so the question does not really arise.

57. GOD'S GRACE
It is not only through our qualities of native strength that God can work. Quite equally and more conspicuously He can make our weakness the opportunity of His grace.

January Twentieth
58. JUSTIFICATION OF FAITH
The question is whether Faith is justified; and philosophers have set themselves to answer this by considering . . . anything and everything in fact except Faith itself. Before a man says his prayers he is to gain permission to do so from a philosophy which, in deciding whether to grant such permission or not, considers everything except those same prayers. What wonder that Faith and Philosophy have tended to drift apart!

59. FAITH INCREASING
You express whatever faith you have already got by your action, especially at critical moments; but you get more faith chiefly by worship.

60. FAITH AND CERTAINTY
From the point of view of religion, not only of the Christian religion, faith is something nobler in its own kind than certainty. For us finite beings in this world that which most of all calls forth our noblest capacities into action is always a hazard of some kind, never a certainty. It is when we are ready to stake our lives on something being so, or to make something so that is not so, that nobility begins to appear in human nature.

16

61. MAN'S CONTRIBUTION

The sin of each man is a new element in the World Process. It is what, being himself, he contributes to it. And its essence is not that he is a self, but that being a self he is self-centred. What matters to him bulks larger in his estimate of value than what matters equally or even more to others.

62. SIN AND THE GLORY OF GOD

St. Paul's definition of sin is "falling short of the glory of God." It is quite impossible to estimate the amount of harm done by our habitual limitation of the use of the word "sin" to deliberate wrong-doing. Everything about us is sin if it is not what God wants it to be.

63. SELF-CENTREDNESS ON THE GRAND SCALE

And yet when all is said, advance which comes as continuous progress is an expansion of the circle of which self is still the centre. It may theoretically be so expanded as to include all mankind, even all spiritual beings. But self is still the centre, and if God Himself be included in the circle, He is peripheral, not central; He is, for me, my God, not God whose I am.

January Twenty-second

64. MORALS AND MOTIVE OF FEAR

Fear is the most self-centred of all emotions, and the use of it as a constant moral appeal can only make us more self-centred, and therefore must defeat the very object it is desired to attain.

65. COSTLINESS OF REDEMPTION

What would be immoral on God's part, and demoralising to us, would be that He should say to us concerning all our selfishness and nastiness, "Oh, never mind; come along; let us still be friends." . . . He would be below the level of our own consciences. But no one who has received his pardon from the lips of Christ on the Cross is going to think that God says, "Never mind," or that He does not Himself mind. That is how He minds.

66. Not Progress, but Redemption

The motive of love can never operate in full power so long as the motive of self-interest is active at all . . . while on the other side the self-regarding motive can only be extirpated in the abandonment of love, for indeed that abandonment and that extirpation are one thing. The entanglement is complete. . . . Man cannot meet his own deepest need, nor find for himself release from his profoundest trouble. What he needs is not progress, but redemption. If the Kingdom of God is to come on earth, it must be because God first comes on earth Himself.

January Twenty-third

67. Faith and Eternal Life

The life of faith does not earn eternal Life; it is eternal Life. And Christ is its vehicle.

68. Communion of Saints

For if eternity is a mere everlastingness, that for the isolated finite mind would be intolerable. The finite self is constituted in very large measure by its social relationships, and only attains to real unity or to self-consciousness through those relationships. To exist in isolation from them would be spiritual death.

69. Heaven and Hell

Objectively regarded, Heaven and Hell may well be identical. Each is the realisation that Man is utterly subject to the purpose of Another—of God who is Love. To the godly and unselfish soul that is Joy unspeakable; to the selfish soul it is a misery against which he rebels in vain. Heaven and Hell are the two extreme terms of our possible reactions to the Gospel of the Love of God.

January Twenty-fourth

70. Damnation

God must assuredly abolish sin; and if the sinner so sinks himself in his sin as to become truly identified with it, God must destroy him also. And this destruction is no painless swooning out of existence. The complacent sinner need not hope for that. Evil is a principle of division. The soul which is altogether evil would be one which cannot find itself even in its own nature; it is torn with an agony of self-diremption and perishes in a torture of moral insanity. That possibility remains for man as a free personality.

71. "Endless Torment in Hell"

Are there not, however, many passages in the New Testament which speak of the endless torment of the lost? No; as far as my knowledge goes there is none at all. There are sayings which speak of being cast into undying fire. But if we do not approach these with the presupposition that what is thus cast in is indestructible, we shall get the impression, not that it will burn for ever, but that it will be destroyed.

72. "Unending Torment"

Can there be Paradise for any while there is Hell, conceived as unending torment, for some? Each supposedly damned soul was born into the world as a mother's child, and Paradise cannot be Paradise for her if her child is in such a Hell.

January Twenty-fifth

73. Injustice

It is better that thousands should die in tumults rather than that order should be preserved at the cost of injustice voluntarily done to one innocent man. For the suffering and death of the body does not involve deterioration of character; but that injustice should be inflicted on innocence is an outrage on the sanctity of personality, while voluntarily to inflict it is to repudiate that sanctity and the obligations which it imposes.

74. Knowledge of Character

It is always in dealing with persons as persons that personality most truly expresses itself. It tells us something about a man's character if we know that he rises from bed every day at the same hour; it tells us much more about him if we know that he even once rose a great deal earlier to do some act of kindness.

75. Community

Outside the works, physically weary and nervously jaded by monotony, the workman still finds no real community. In the modern big town human beings are jostling atoms, and each must fend for himself.

January Twenty-sixth

76. Tennyson
I am not a great admirer of Tennyson as a poet, apart from the shorter lyrics.

77. Detective Stories
Of course the essence of a detective story is that it is a kind of game in which the pleasure consists in being beaten; if you spot the criminal before the end, it rather spoils your pleasure.

78. Books
One suggestion which has been made, and which I most heartily endorse, is that we should urge the provision in all new houses of built-in bookshelves, so that those who do buy books will not be faced with what may be for them the really vexatious alternatives of either buying bookshelves, which it may be difficult to afford, or of leaving the books lying about untidily.

January Twenty-seventh

79. Freedom
Freedom is not absence of determination; it is spiritual determination, as distinct from mechanical or even organic determination. It is determination by what seems good as contrasted with determination by irresistible compulsion.

80. Locus of Freedom
The locus of freedom is the personality as a whole, but rather the life of thought than of will, so far as will is conceived as active in particular choices of alternative modes of conduct. Hence comes the profound significance of St. Paul's counsel: "Whatsoever things are true . . . occupy your minds with these things."

81. Spiritual Freedom
True spiritual freedom would be the state of a man who, knowing an ideal which completely satisfied all aspects of his nature, always

in fact conformed to it and could perfectly trust himself so to do. . . . Yet it differs from freedom of choice because there is no selection between alternative courses of action regarded as equally possible.

January Twenty-eighth

82. THE VEHICLE OF FULL REVELATION

In nature we find God; we do not only infer from Nature what God must be like, but when we see Nature truly, we see God self-manifested in and through it. Yet the self-revelation so given is incomplete and inadequate. Personality can only reveal itself in persons. Consequently it is specially in Human Nature—in men and women—that we see God.

83. MIND AND NATURE

From the play of minutest particles to the sweep of stars in their courses, the work of Mind is found—of a Mind so mighty in range and scope, so sure in adjustment of infinitesimal detail, that before it all our science is clumsy and precarious.

84. SIGNIFICANCE OF HUMAN APPREHENSION

Quite as impressive as the vastness of the universe or the infinite delicacy of its articulation is the apprehension of these qualities by beings who, from one point of view, are mere episodes of its continually changing process.

January Twenty-ninth

85. KEEPING A PROMISE

It is not because "a promise is a promise" that a man must keep it at great inconvenience to himself and even to others. It is because a promise creates a personal claim, and to break it for any reason which the man to whom it was made cannot be expected to regard as compelling, is to ignore his claim and so to flout the sanctity of his personality.

86. RIGHT AND WRONG

The variety of ethical codes in different parts of the world pre-supposes agreement in one thing, namely, that there is a difference between right and wrong. People may call some things right in some parts of the world which are called wrong in another part of the world; but the difference between right and wrong remains.

87. STANDARD OF MORALS PASSED

The standard of morals is the mind of Christ; that is our great principle if we are Christian. It will not help you at once to solve each particular problem; it will give you a touch-stone. . . . Your moral authority is not a principle, but a Person. It is the mind of Christ.

January Thirtieth

88. NO EARTHLY PERFECTION

We must work and pray for the coming of God's Kingdom on earth; and every new assertion of God's Authority over His world is sheer gain; yet we must also recognise that the Kingdom cannot come in its perfection within the period of human history and under its conditions.

89. KINGDOM OF GOD ACTUAL NOW

Is the Divine Kingdom something which will be actual in the future but has no actuality now? Assuredly not. In the course of individual lives and in the history of nations, God asserts His sovereignty by the judgments which follow neglect of His law.

90. KINGDOM OF GOD

Those who have given their lives for the Kingdom of God have never felt that they were making their sacrifice for a dream of their own, but in order to bring into present actuality what is after its own manner already profoundly real.

January Thirty-first

91. LOVE'S EXPRESSION

The greatest thing that can happen to any human soul is to become utterly filled with love; and self-sacrifice is love's natural expression.

92. LOVE AND SPONTANEITY

With man, love means that you like being with them, are glad when you do what pleases them, and sorry when you do what pains them. The love of God means just that. And when you love, you do not laboriously think out and perform the will of the beloved; you wish to please him, and largely, at least, trust to your spontaneous sense of what will do this. That may begin to be true and become increasingly true of our service of God, just in the degree in which we genuinely set ourselves to live in the constant companionship of our Lord.

93. ACTUAL VALUE

A man may be of a loving disposition, but he actually loves only when another persons exists to be the object of his love; and then the love is in him, not in the occasion of its actualisation; so, turning from active to passive, the picture is always admirable; but the value of this is actual only when it is admired.

FEBRUARY

February First

94. INCARNATION: NEWS ABOUT GOD

The doctrine of the Incarnation is not first and foremost of importance because of what it says about Somebody who lived in Palestine; it is of fundamental importance because of what it tells us about the eternal and unchanging God, who is and always will be Himself.

95. UNION WITH GOD

We come closest to God not when, with our mind, we obtain a wide conspectus of truth, but when in our purposes we are united with His righteous purpose.

96. LIMITATIONS OF DOCTRINE

The doctrine of the universal Sovereignty of the divine will is paralysing so long as it is doctrine only; but when it is matter of personal experience, it becomes impulse and energy and inspiration.

February Second

97. PRE-EXISTENT SON

The Second Person of the Blessed Trinity was no less *in heaven* during the period of the earthly ministry than either before or after it. What we see as we watch the life of Jesus is the very life of heaven—indeed of God—in human expression.

98. LIGHT OF THE WORLD

Christ the Light of the World shines first upon the soul, and then from within the soul upon the path of life. He does not illumine our way while leaving us unconverted; but by converting us He illumines our way.

99. CHRIST AND ASCETICISM

In His human life He was unmarried, and truly detached from earthly ties; He had His own special mission, the specifically universal mission, for the discharge of which He must be free from all particular commitments and the obligations resulting from them. At first He directed His followers to practise a similar detachment, as in the charge to the Twelve before their first mission (Matthew x). But later, when the things concerning Him had fulfilment, He deliberately countermanded this (Luke xxii.36, 37).

February Third

100. HOLY SPIRIT AND DAILY LIFE
The Holy Spirit is the Person in the Trinity with whom we are most constantly in conscious contact.

101. RESPONSIVE ASPIRATION
Holy Spirit was hardly recognised as distinct from the Word until the Word was uttered in a new fullness of expression, as Christians believe, in the historical Person, Jesus of Nazareth. That fuller objective manifestation of the divine called forth a new potency of responsive aspiration to which, as an experienced fact, was given the name Holy Spirit.

102. HOLY SPIRIT'S MOVEMENT
Whenever a man feels called upon to neglect his natural interests or his animal desires in the service of any sort of ideal whatsoever, there you have the movement of the Holy Spirit.

February Fourth

103. CHURCH INFLUENCE
We have to remember that many of the fruits of the Church's existence and activity are to be found entirely outside its own specific organisation; for wherever you find the Spirit of Christ gaining hold among men, there you see the result of the continual activity of the Church across the ages.

104. RENEWAL OF LIFE IN THE CHURCH
Remember, the supreme wonder of the history of the Christian Church is that always in the moments when it has seemed most dead, out of its own body there has sprung up new life; so that in age after age it has renewed itself, and age after age by its renewal has carried the world forward into new stages of progress,

as it will do for us in our day, if only we give ourselves in devotion to its Lord and take our place in its service.

105. CHURCH ORDER GIVEN

Where Church Order is not accepted as a thing given, as distinct from a thing to be constructed, there is often a reluctance to accept the Revelation in Christ as a thing given, or to receive the life of fellowship with God as a thing given. In spite of Luther and Calvin, some branches of Protestantism have developed a degree of Pelagianism which is to my mind inconceivable in Churches of the historic Order.

February Fifth

106. STUDY OF WORSHIP

A man who is colour-blind may master the science of optics, he may be as competent as anyone else to follow discussions of rival theories of light, but he will never see a sunset as others see it, and his appreciation of a poetic description of it is bound to be sadly limited. So the man, who studies the worship of others but is not himself a worshipper, may discuss with clarity and insight the grounds which prompt men to worship, or which lead them to a sense of sin and its forgiveness; but what those tidings are in themselves and in their pervasive influence on experience as a whole, he can never know unless he learns to worship.

107. CONDUCT AND WORSHIP

People are always thinking that conduct is supremely important, and that because prayer helps it, therefore prayer is good. That is true as far as it goes; still truer is it to say that worship is of supreme importance and conduct tests it. Conduct tests how much of yourself was in the worship you gave to God.

108. WORSHIP, DEFINITION

What worship means is the submission of the whole being to the object of worship. It is the opening of the heart to receive the love of God; it is the subjection of conscience to be directed by Him; it is the declaration of need to be fulfilled by Him; it is the subjection of desire to be controlled by Him; and, as the result of all these together, it is the surrender of will to be used by Him. It is the total giving of self.

February Sixth

109. SELF-FORGETFULNESS IN PRAYER

You get most help from religion when you have stopped thinking about your needs, even for spiritual strength, and think about God. Gaze and gaze on Him.

110. USING WORDS IN PRAYER

Remember that the only object of using words in your prayers is to fix your own thoughts, not to give information to God. He can read your thoughts, but your thoughts are likely to be very vague and wandering unless you fix them by means of words. It is for your own sake, not for God's, that you put your prayers into words. That being so, in your private prayers, those are the right words which succeed in fixing your thoughts on the right objects. . . . The words that help you are the right words for you to use.

111. FAITH IN PRAYER

Your confidence in praying ought not to be chiefly confidence that you are going to get what you ask, because that will be confidence as much in your own judgment as in God. . . . You must pass from faith that God will give you what you ask, to faith that what He gives is better than what you asked.

February Seventh

112. POETRY

When a poet takes words as his instruments, the very sound of the words is now part of the meaning; that meaning can never be apprehended or recovered except by re-hearing physically or in imagination the actual sound of the words. . . . Here we are near to a sacrament.

113. AUTHORITY TO ADMINISTER SACRAMENTS

What is conferred in Ordination is not the power to make sacramental a rite which otherwise would not be such, but *authority* (*potestas*) to administer Sacraments which belong to the Church, and which, therefore, can only be rightly administered by those who hold the Church's commission to do so.

114. ORDINATION AND SACRAMENTS

It is necessary to be clear on whether we regard the action of the
Church in Ordination as so related to the Sacraments that where
there is no episcopally ordained priest there is no real Sacrament.
I find that position untenable, and even in the last resort unin-
telligible.

February Eighth

115. REVELATION LIMITLESS

Unless all things are revelation, nothing can be revelation. Unless
the rising of the sun reveals God, the rising of the Son of Man from
the dead cannot reveal God.

116. CONDITIONS OF REVELATION

The conditions of the possibility of any revelation require that
there should be nothing which is not revelation. Only if God is
revealed in the rising of the sun in the sky can He be revealed in
the rising of a son of man from the dead; only if He is revealed
in the history of Syrians and Philistines can He be revealed in the
history of Israel; only if He chooses all men for His own can He
choose any at all; only if nothing is profane can anything be
sacred.

117. THE MIND OF THE PROPHET

The prophet is primarily the man, not to whom God has communicated certain divine thoughts, but whose mind is illuminated
by the divine spirit to interpret aright the divine acts; and the act
is primary.

February Ninth

118. AGNOSTICISM

In view of the place which Religion has held in the experience of
mankind, it is no more reasonable for any individual to adopt in
practice a negative attitude towards religion on the ground that
he has not proved for himself the reality of its object, than it is
to adopt a positive attitude because he has not disproved it.

119. RATIONALITY AND GOD

To prove that the world is a rational whole in such sense as to
make scientific procedure possible, and then to call its attribute

of rationality by the name of God, is a course of argumentation in which much dialectical skill may be displayed, but it does not establish the existence of such a Being as can satisfy man's age-long search for God.

120. LIMITATION OF MATTER

What some of our modern scientific thinkers are feeling is that the world is so vast that we cannot very much matter in it; and yet I know the stars are there, and if they are nothing more than Sir James Jeans has found out about them, they do not know I am here. I beat the stars.

February Tenth

121. BEAUTY SHARED

Even knowledge and beauty are heightened when they are shared, and, in the common enjoyment, provide a link uniting the two personalities together in a relationship which most people find more precious than the experience which united them.

122. BEAUTY CONCEALED

We are repelled by the ugliness of a modern industrial town, until some artist reveals the beauty of strong stark lines in factory chimneys, or of sweeping curves in a gasometer. This does not mean that what we had thought ugly is really beautiful, but rather that there is beauty present in it, and concealed in it until it is detected by a rightly directed and rightly concentrated attention.

123. MEANING OF THE ARTIST

We must be careful in speaking of the "meaning" of an artist or of a work of art; that meaning is not something that can be expressed in a proposition; it requires for its expression the whole work of art. It is impossible to say what is the meaning of *King Lear* or the Mass in B Minor; Shakespeare and Bach have expressed those meanings in the only possible way.

February Eleventh

124. RELATIVITY AND TRUTH

The doctrine of relativity is in no sense whatever hostile to the conception of absolute truth; on the contrary, it claims to be itself absolutely true.

125. PSYCHOLOGY AND TRUTH

The question of truth is, after all, paramount even for psychology; for the theory that my beliefs are all to be accounted for by my personal history is advanced, if at all, only on the supposition that it is true. But belief in that theory has a history in the life of the psychologist who holds it as much as my belief in God has a history in mine. If the psychological account of our beliefs is all that can be said about them, that is as damaging to psychological beliefs as to the theological.

126. "REVEALED TRUTH"

There is no such thing as revealed truth. There are truths of revelation, that is to say, propositions which express the results of correct thinking concerning revelation; but they are not themselves directly revealed.

February Twelfth

127. THE NATURE OF THE GOOD

Good or bad consists in the discovery by the mind of what is akin to or alien from itself in the thing it contemplates. Wherever you find the nature of mind answering your mind, there you have satisfaction.

128. ANALYSIS OF "OBLIGATION"

If any man . . . thinks that the consciousness of obligation can be analysed without remainder into a spontaneous tendency to act in conformity with the customs of his social context, he must be left to think so; but it is hard on that hypothesis to understand why the most imperative demands of conscience are demands that the individual should defy his social context.

129. GOODNESS IN SCIENTIST AND ARTIST

I do not think you can say that a man who is devoting all his faculties to science will be a better scientist if he becomes a Christian, though he will be a more complete man. I should find it hard to say that an artist would necessarily become a better artist by becoming a Christian, though I should expect it to result in some greater refinement in his art.

33

February Thirteenth

130. GUILTY ACQUIESCENCE

If under pressure from vested interests the State pursues a policy involving injustice or a plain denial of equal fellowship, the Church which silently acquiesces is rightly discredited.

131. TOTALITARIAN JUSTICE

The totalitarian States define justice as that treatment of the individual which most conduces to the welfare of the State. What the welfare of the State may be is not, so far as I know, anywhere defined. It would certainly include, and perhaps would chiefly consist in, the power of the State to maintain its will against other States and to impose its will upon them. But then we need to ask what its will is, and why it is this. When we press home the Totalitarian doctrines they are found to be in a high degree self-contradictory.

132. STATE AND MAN'S DESTINY

If man is indeed destined for eternal life in fellowship with God, that is a fact so important in his whole nature that the State must take note of it, and have a care that the facts of life which fall under its own control are not so ordered as to hinder the citizens from qualifying for their eternal destiny.

February Fourteenth

133. VOCATION IN DAILY WORK

Whatever the work you do for your living, it must be a form of service of some kind, for no one will pay you for your work if he does not want it done. What makes all the difference is what you are thinking of first and foremost as you consider the spirit and temper in which you carry out your work. Is it your livelihood or is it God's service? The work in itself is both. But which do you think of first? Nothing would bring nearer the promised day of God than that all Christian people should enter on their profession in the spirit of those who regard it as their chief sphere of serving God.

134. PRAYER AND OUR DAILY WORK

There ought to be no sense of spiritual transition as we pass from any occupation which is our proper occupation at the time to the thought of God. We should feel, whether it be in performing the duty He has given us or in remembering Him who gave us the duty, that we are always seeking to deepen our union with Him. But the moments when we concentrate upon this purpose particularly are our times of prayer.

135. Competition in Commerce
When personal immunity from attack is secured, the question arises whether cut-throat competition is not in the same category of disorder as the cutting of throats. It can reasonably be claimed that the evil conditions in factories immediately after the Industrial Revolution were acute forms of disorder, and that Lord Shaftesbury's Factory Acts were passed for the establishment and maintenance of reasonable order in that sphere.

February Fifteenth

136. Sex in Man
Sex, being a strong natural appetite in animals, and being enormously strengthened in man by the use of imagination, is very liable in human nature to grow in a degree entirely disproportionate. So there is a peculiar difficulty in maintaining, in this respect, that true economy of nature in which to every impulse there is given its own proper, but no more than its own proper, exercise. If our ancestors were wrong in their suggestions that there was about sex something wrong, they were quite right in thinking there was about it something which gave the greatest ground for the most anxious caution.

137. Sacredness of Sex
It is to be recognised that sex is holy as well as wholesome. . . . It is the means by which we may co-operate with God in bringing into the world children of His own destined for eternal life. Anyone, who has once understood that, will be quite as careful as any Puritan to avoid making jokes about sex; not because it is nasty, but because it is sacred. He would no more joke about sex than he would joke about the Holy Communion—and for exactly the same reason. To joke about it is to treat with lightness something that deserves reverence.

138. Contraception

The deliberate avoidance of parenthood is an outrage on the whole conception of marriage; and the deliberate postponement of parenthood after marriage is so gravely objectionable in all but the very rarest cases, and is in all cases so perilous, that the Church should in its teaching give most solemn warning against it.

February Sixteenth

139. Reason and Guidance

Over and over again it will happen that if a man, having thought out a problem to the best of his ability, will then lay the whole matter in the hands of God, and genuinely desire that God's Will shall be done in his life and not his own, he will become perfectly clear what that will is. Over and over again that happens.

140. Futile Prayers

We use His Name, but do not stop to think what it means. Our minds are focused on the things we ask for, and not upon God. That is not praying; that is uttering wishes to no one in particular. I cannot imagine anything more tedious or more futile. Naturally, people who get fixed in that habit say they find their prayers are no good, so they give them up. What they were doing was no good; it was not praying.

141. Three Elements in Petitionary Prayer

In our Lord's teaching about petitionary prayer there are three main principles. The first is confidence, the second is perseverance, and the third, for lack of a better word, I will call correspondence with Christ.

February Seventeeth

142. Eucharistic Oblations

In the Eucharist we bring familiar forms of economic wealth . . . and offer them as symbols of our earthly life. If God had not given to the seed its life and to the soil the quality to nurture it, there would be neither harvest nor bread. Equally, if man had not ploughed the soil and scattered the seed, there would be neither harvest nor bread. Bread is a product of man's labour exercised upon God's gift for the satisfaction of man's need. So is wine. These are our "oblations" at the "offertory"—often also accompanied by "alms" expressing the charity which seeks to share with others the good things which God has given to us.

143. EUCHARISTIC SELF-OFFERING

These representatives of all earthly "goods" we offer to God in union with the act of Christ in the Last Supper when, in preparatory interpretation of His death, He took the bread, called it His Body, and broke it—took the wine, called it His Blood, and gave it. Because we have offered our "earthly" goods to God, He gives them back to us as heavenly goods, binding us into union with Christ in that self-offering which is His royalty, so that we give not only our goods but ourselves, and thus become strengthened as members of His Body to do His will in the various departments of our life.

144. EUCHARISTIC EATING AND DRINKING

To "eat the flesh" and to "drink the blood" of the Son of Man are not the same. The former is to receive the power of self-giving, and self-sacrifice to the uttermost. The latter is to receive, in and through that self-giving and self-sacrifice, the life that is triumphant over death and united to God.

February Eighteenth

145. CHURCH: FELLOWSHIP OR ASSOCIATION

Has the Church lost the distinctive quality of true Fellowship—a union of all through the control of each by one Spirit—and become an Association, a voluntary organisation of persons concerned to provide satisfaction for their religious appetites and those of others? As such an Association the State inevitably regards it. For the State all groupings are compulsory or voluntary; and on that basis of division, the Church is voluntary. The pity is that it so largely lives and works at that level. Then it becomes as self-defensive as any other human association. It interprets the confiscation of its property as an attack upon itself, and tries, as mediæval Popes habitually tried, to throw the protection of the sanctity to which it is called over the property which it has acquired.

146. GOING TO CHURCH

If you ever catch yourself saying, "I got no good from it, so I gave up going," remember that only proves you were coming in the frame of mind in which you were not likely to get much good.

147. OBEDIENCE TO THE CHURCH

Though mere obedience to the Church may be spiritual in principle, and may even be the best and wisest course for many individuals, yet it is a limitation of the area of full spiritual response, and if all questions were regarded as settled by the Church, the exercise of spiritual faculty would be very disastrously curtailed for its members.

February Nineteenth

148. THE GRACE OF GOD

While it cannot without spiritual disaster be contended that man apart from God is free to do the will of God, it is also indispensable to faith and to morality to hold that God empowers men to do His will through the enlightenment of their natural faculties and the kindling of their natural affections, and not by any supersession of these.

149. CALLED BY THE FATHER

To realise that my not "coming" is itself due to the will of the Father, who has not yet drawn me, and to accept this, is one beginning of trust in Him, one sign that in fact He is really drawing me to come. And then there is safety.

150. GOD'S INITIATIVE

The drawing of the Father is not a mechanical impulsion in which our wills play no part; the "drawing" is effected by the influence of the word spoken on our hearts and minds. We cannot hear unless the Father speaks; all initiative lies with Him; but when we hear it lies with us (sustained by His grace) to learn or not to learn.

February Twentieth

151. RELIGION AND FAITH

Surely we are disproportionately concerned about religion, and not enough about faith. Religion is an affair of the human soul, and in it emotion plays a great part; it is of inestimable value, and quite indispensable; yet in itself, as distinguished from the religious habit of mind, as a whole, it remains departmental.

152. FAITH ALL-PERVASIVE

Religion, as an activity of meditation, cannot rightly occupy more than a small part of the time of most members of the community. The proportions suggested by the Fourth Commandment are one to six. But faith can be, and should be, pervasive of all life; for a man may plough the field having perfect trust in God in his heart and yet give his whole attention to driving his furrow straight and turning his corner well.

153. FAITH OBJECTIVE

For faith is always intensely objective. The emphasis in the Creed is on the fourth word, not on the first two, which for that reason, should never be used alone in introducing it. It is not my state of mind that matters most, even to me, but God.

February Twenty-first

154. SIN: NOT CERTAIN BUT LIKELY

That the finite mind, rooted as it is in a physiological organism, should at first find its apparent good in what gratifies itself and brings comfort to the organism is "too probable not to happen," though not strictly necessary; for it is possible without contradiction to conceive a mind which from the outset chose the general good as its own. Inasmuch as finitude does not necessarily involve self-centredness, it cannot be said that the very principle of the actual creation involved sin.

155. SIN AS OCCASION OF TRIUMPH

At long last, we may hope, every sinner—even Judas Iscariot and every traitor with him—shall be so purged of self-concern by the very shame which his offence has caused to that same self-concern,

39

that he in utter humility will thank God that his vileness has become a further occasion of the divine triumph.

156. CORRUPTION OF THE GOOD
The evil is a corruption of what can be, and partly is, good. There is selfishness in the world, but also love. There is greed in the world, but also self-discipline. There is avarice in the world, but also generosity. Actual human history and civilisation are carried forward and moulded by each of these.

February Twenty-second

157. SALVATION AND SELF-INTEREST
No one who is convinced of his own salvation is as yet even safe, let alone "saved." Salvation is the state of him who has ceased to be interested whether he is saved or not, provided that what takes the place of that supreme self-interest is not a lower form of self-interest but the glory of God.

158. FEAR AND SALVATION
The fear of future pain or of destruction may stimulate a man for his own self's sake to seek salvation; but the only salvation that exists or can exist is one that he can never find while he seeks it for his own self's sake.

159. SUBSTITUTION AND REDEMPTION
By His suffering, our Lord did make it possible for us to avoid suffering continual alienation from God and the consequences of this; and therefore, in a sense, His suffering is substituted for ours; but it is not a transferred penalty; it is something in the nature of a price paid; it is something which He gave, by means of which we are set free. It is a real redemption; but what He is concerned with all the time is delivering us, not from the consequences of sin, but from sin; and the centre of sin is self. So He is delivering us out of self-centredness into a life that finds its centre in God.

February Twenty-third

160. PSEUDO-RELIGIOUS ESCAPISM

The Christian doctrine is a doctrine of Eternal Life; not of Immortality but of Resurrection. The difference is profound. The method of all non-Christian systems is to seek an escape from the evils and misery of life. Christianity seeks no escape, but accepts these at their worst, and makes them the material of its triumphant joy. That is the special significance in this connection of the Cross and Resurrection of Jesus Christ.

161. CONDITIONAL IMMORTALITY

The prevailing doctrine of the New Testament, as I think, is that God alone is immortal, being in His own Nature eternal; and that He offers immortality to men not universally but conditionally.

162. IMPLICATIONS OF HISTORY

The historical is of significance and importance to the eternal inasmuch as the eternal is such as to create it, so that if it were not created that would prove the eternal to be other than, in the light of its creativity, it is known to be.

163. ETERNAL LIFE

The presentation of the Gospel to the worldly minded always suffers under this disability, that the world confidently believes it to be something quite different from what it is. It cannot "see" it. . . . So men think of eternal life as the everlasting happiness of a still self-centred soul. But it is nothing of the kind. It is fellowship with God in which our souls, so far as they are self-centred, can find no happiness.

February Twenty-fourth

164. EVERLASTING TORMENT

I am not going to say anything about the bewildering subject of the ultimate fate of the soul which refuses the love of God. On the one side it seems clear that we have the power to refuse, and He will not override it; on the other side there are those who say that, in respect of a soul that finally rejects His love, Almighty God has failed; and that is inconceivable. There, I think, we must leave it, recognising that it is the kind of problem which peculiarly belongs to the eternal world, and is therefore not likely to be open to complete solution here. But one thing we can say with confidence; everlasting torment is to be ruled out. . . . It is the fire that is called æonian, not the life cast into it. But what the New Testament does most surely teach is the reality of "abiding consequences" of all we do.

165. HELL
Everlasting life for the isolated soul is neither possible nor (for anyone who knows what he is talking about) desirable; so far as it could occur, it would be hell.

166. EVERLASTING PUNISHMENT
Annihilation is an everlasting punishment, though it is not unending torment.

February Twenty-fifth

167. MEMBERS ONE OF ANOTHER
The child who is sorry to see his mother in pain does not wish that pain away in order to end his own sorrow; what he resents is not his sorrow but her pain. In other words, we are from the beginning, and by the very constitution of our nature, bound up with one another, so that the weal and woe of each is in itself the weal and woe of all others within the circle of intimate relationships.

168. ORGANISED SELFISHNESS
An attempt to organise life on a basis of selfishness would lead to a social order in which each individual would in fact conform to the requirements of the common good, even though only from selfish motives.

169. THE SPIRITUALLY-MINDED MAN
The spiritually-minded man does not differ from the materially-minded man chiefly in thinking about different things, but in thinking about the same things differently. It is possible to think materially about God, and spiritually about food.

February Twenty-sixth

170. REAL FREEDOM

As consciousness develops into mind with its free ideas, choice becomes possible, not only as between means to a fixed end (such as the satisfaction of an appetite) but between alternative and incompatible ends (as between duty and pleasure). Only at this stage is there real freedom.

171. OMNIPOTENCE AND FREE WILL

If God exercised compulsion by forcing obedience or by remaking the character of a self against its will, He would have abandoned omnipotence in the act which should assert it, for the will that was overridden would remain outside His control.

172. FREEDOM OF RESPONSE

If Christ had written a code of precepts or a manual of theology, those who accepted Him as the Incarnate Self-Utterance of the Eternal God might have found it impossible to deviate from what was so laid down. But in doing this He would have confined the fully spiritual response of His followers to their general acceptance of Him as Lord. . . . The purely spiritual authority of the revelation is secured by the removal of what would otherwise have been the almost coercive quality of its divine origin.

February Twenty-seventh

173. THE CONDITION OF PROGRESS

The most indispensable condition of moral responsibility is that you should know which way to go. If you are always changing your direction, you never get any farther, and one reason why the last fifty years have been so barren of effective political progress is that people have been constantly changing their direction. . . . "I am the way," said Christ, and what is offered is not the goal of history, but the direction in which history should move, and the power which should carry it forward.

174. GENERAL MORAL RULES

There are no general negative rules about morals which are fit for universal acceptance, unless they are so formed as to include reference to motive or to particular conditions. For example, we may be content to say that murder is always wrong, but that is because murder is a kind of killing which is wrong. But not all killing is wrong.

175. TEN COMMANDMENTS

The primitive ethical codes of all nations are mainly negative. That is because people . . . have, by long experience, found out that this, that, and the other actions are not compatible with it. That is how the negative rules, such as we have in most of the Decalogue, get built up. They are the deposit of the accumulated experience of the tribe or race regarding its experience that such and such courses of conduct do, in fact, result in disaster if they are permitted to become frequent in society.

February Twenty-eighth

176. APPEARANCE OF MIND

We do not have to ask how Mind effects a transition from its own ideas to an objective world, because we see Mind first appearing as the consciousness of processes which had been going on in the physical world before that appearance.

177. INDEPENDENCE OF THE MIND

As mind increasingly takes control of the organism, so it becomes increasingly independent of the organism as physiologically conceived. A man may be so absorbed in thought as to become insensitive to occurrences that would usually occasion severe pain. In some such cases a degree of detachment is achieved which would have antecedently been pronounced by fully competent judges to be impossible.

178. THE USE OF FREE IDEAS

By use of its capacity for free ideas, mind conceives situations for its organism which do not exist, and directs the energies of the organism towards bringing these into existence. Thus are initiated moral action and responsibility, art, science and every form of deliberate progress.

179. Kingdom of God and Love

The Kingdom of God is the Sovereignty of Love—since God is Love. That great proclamation brings comfort and courage to all whose hearts are attuned to it; for if God is Love, then Love is the ultimate power of the universe, and every purpose or policy prompted by Love—by the desire to serve rather than to gain—will reach its fulfilment, whatever the sacrifices that may first be required of it, because it is allied with the supreme power.

180. Kingship of Jesus

Once, and only once, our Lord applied to Himself the title of King; that was when He identified Himself with the outcasts and the failures of society. "Then shall the King say unto them. . . . I was an-hungered and ye gave me meat . . . I was in prison and ye came unto me."

181. The Kingdom and Repentance

The completion of our repentance and the coming of the kingdom are not cause and effect; they are the same thing viewed from different sides.

MARCH

March First

182. READING THE GOSPELS

Our reading of the Gospel story can be and should be an act of personal communion with the living Lord.

183. BELIEVING AND BELIEVING IN THE GOSPEL

When a man is both orthodox and self-assertive, believing the Gospel but not believing in it—a very familiar spiritual state—he is not recognising and making acquaintance with the truth. . . . He may preach the Gospel of redemption to others, and never know that he needs it himself. Pharisaism is not an exclusively Jewish phenomenon.

184. BELIEVING THE GOSPEL

If a man cannot believe the Gospel at all, it may be that some new presentation of it may carry it past all obstacles to reach his conscience, heart, and mind. But if he does believe it, yet fails to put practical trust in Him whom it presents, there is some fatal influence at work in opposition. And how many of us fall, wholly or in part, under that description.

March Second

185. RESPONSE TO CHRIST

Christ stimulates us, as other great men stimulate us, but we find a power coming from Him into our lives that enables us to respond. That is the experience that proves Him to be the universal Spirit. It does not happen with others.

186. PRESENTING CHRIST

We tend at first to admire rather self-conscious and strutting heroes, because that is the kind of heroism to which we ourselves aspire. It is our apparent good. And for a time such an ideal may satisfy. Then one day we see Bombastes Furioso confronted by some great gentleman, and the bubble is pricked. There is the latent capacity to admire true goodness and greatness, if only it

49

be presented in a form that we can really see. . . . "The highest" must be presented in a form adapted to our capacity to see.

187. EARTHLY SUCCESS

We want Him to accompany us (so to speak) on some enterprise, and to vindicate what is said on His behalf by us or by others through the signal success that He enables us to win. But we are left in fact to toil on with no glad sense of His presence as our companion; and at the end we find Him awaiting us with the Prophet's rebuke for our defect of wisdom or of loyalty; when we have Him again with us it is not as the encouraging fellow traveller, but as the Judge condemning the faults which unfit us for His service.

March Third

188. SCIENTIFIC METHOD

The simple and plain fact is that the scientific method wins its success by ignoring parts of reality as given in experience; it is perfectly right to do this for its own purposes; but it must not be permitted by a kind of bluff to create the impression that what it ignores is non-existent.

189. DETERMINISM

To suppose that a physiological organism becomes conscious only because its own evolution has brought it to a certain stage of complexity would be like supposing that the mechanical robot at a street corner will automatically turn into a policeman if the traffic is sufficiently congested.

190. NATURAL LAW

The behaviour of Nature according to "Law" is no less a manifestation of the Mind of God, and thus an utterance of His Word, than its unpredictable behaviour from moment to moment would be.

March Fourth

191. ANIMAL LEVEL

Where a man chooses comfort as his "good" he is in fact choosing to remain at the animal level when he has capacity for more.

192. DOING LITTLE UNITEDLY

But when we come to what we can do ourselves, it always seems so little, as, of course, it is. What each one alone can do is always very little, but the way great things are done is by all doing that very little unitedly.

193. THE RELIGIOUS MAN

It is not religious experiences, but religious experience as a whole, that is of chief concern. For the religious man is not only religious when he prays; his work is religiously done, his recreation religiously enjoyed, his food and drink religiously received; the last he often emphasises by the custom of "grace before meat."

March Fifth

194. ZEAL FOR RIGHTEOUSNESS

Who shall say that zeal for righteousness is in God's sight less pleasing than completeness of sacramental Order?

195. REAL PRESENCE

The "Real Presence" in the Eucharist is a fact, but it is not unique. The Word of God is everywhere present and active. The Bread and Wine have a symbolic meaning before they are consecrated—they are the gift of God rendered serviceable by the labour of man.

196. RITES AND UNIVERSAL FELLOWSHIP

Feeling and conscious realisation are greatly to be welcomed when they spring out of the due performance of the appointed rite. But they must not be made the basis of the rite, if only for the reason that the rite essentially stands for a fellowship qualified to be universal, while every fellowship based on human sympathy has narrow limits.

March Sixth

197. CONDUCT IN WORSHIP

It is mere humbug to say that we will serve God by our conduct but cannot find time for prayer and worship. If that is all we can do, we shall serve Him just as much as we have been doing—which is what has brought the world to the mess it is now in. We must have our times for companionship with God.

198. Spontaneous Judgments

In his leisure a man should criticise his conscience by reflection, and discipline his character by meditation; but at the moment for action he must act, being what he is, and knowing that his spontaneous judgments, however much they still need correction, have the authority of the garnered experience of the race.

199. Meditation

I am the light of the world. It is useful to look up Light and Darkness in a concordance and use the passages so brought together in meditation.

March Seventh

200. Unity of All State Actions

It is not possible for any State to adopt one set of principles for internal affairs and another for external; for what determines its action in either case is its understanding of human life in general.

201. Sanctions

The use of sanctions may be perfectly justified, provided its aim is to develop a character that will no longer require them; but it must be clearly recognised that sanctions do not become spiritual in virtue of the fact that they are imposed by a spiritual Being or Society; they approximate to the spiritual when they are such as to make a spiritual appeal.

202. Manchurian Incident

It may have been so difficult as to be reckoned impossible to go to the help of China in Manchuria when Japan was formally pronounced guilty of aggression. But we might have avoided putting an embargo on the export of arms to both countries *immediately after* that judgment had been pronounced. That was a very severe slap in the face to the League's authority.

March Eighth

203. The Prophets

The prophets were not Gifford Lecturers with the advantage of some special "guidance." They were men faced with practical problems of political, moral and spiritual life. . . . As the prophet faces some actual human need, that truth of God which bears upon it irradiates his mind and he proclaims it in words that thrill our hearts to-day.

204. Locus of Prophecy

What we have in the prophetical writings of the Old Testament . . . is not a divine message, other than the prophetic utterance itself, which has been distorted into this by the medium through which it has passed. That utterance is the only message, but it comes out of an experience of communion with the divine which endows it with more than human authority, though not with the inerrancy of a divinely dictated oracle.

205. Divine Accommodation

Moses was to convince his people of the authenticity of his mission by the conversion of his staff into a snake. Whether God ever does such things in accommodation to primitive minds is not a question for Natural Theology; if He could want to do it, He could also do it; but the probable explanation of this and similar episodes is to be sought in hypnotism.

March Ninth

206. Christ: the Son of God

He is the Son of God in that sense (among others) in which we say of a man that he is the son of his father, meaning that in him the father's character is reproduced. So supremely is our Lord the Son because in Him we truly see the Father.

207. Propitiation

The Christian who has heard his word of pardon from the lips of Christ upon the Cross is never in danger of supposing that God does not mind. He minds, like that. And so, as St. Paul says, Christ as set forth upon the Cross shows the righteousness of God in the very act of forgiveness. This is part at least of that which Christian tradition has stood for in its insistence that the mere appeal of love to our souls is not sufficient as an account of the Atonement—that there must also be in a true sense a propitiation toward God.

208. "GOD: SAME YESTERDAY . . ."

The death and Resurrection of Christ did not cause God to be after their occurrence what He was not before.

March Tenth

209. CONDITIONS OF FORGIVENESS

You see it makes all the difference in the world whether you come to God saying, "I am truly sorry and I mean never to do it again," or whether you come to God saying, "I am truly sorry, but I have forgiven everyone who has injured me," because in the one case you come as an isolated individual, almost making a claim upon God because you have fulfilled His condition; in the other you come as one member of His family, knowing that you have no claim except what His love grants to all.

210. FORGIVENESS AND FAMILY INTIMACY

The prisoner in the dock has no personal relationship to the judge upon the bench; he does not have to think what pain his misconduct has caused to the judge; all he thinks about is what the judge is going to do to him. It is a poor kind of family life in which that is what the child thinks about the father when the child has given offence. Once there is love, forgiveness does not mean remission of penalty. Penalty does not come in. Forgiveness means restoration to intimacy.

211. CORRUPTED WILL

The fact that you have at all to will that your will should be better than it is, shows that the instrument of your action is itself corrupted. Something must take hold of you from without. You can't do it for yourself. All you can do, and that is possible, is, in moments when the better purpose is uppermost, to submit yourself to the influences which have the transforming power.

March Eleventh

212. A RIGHT ACT

We repudiate the intuitionism which holds that right and wrong are inherent qualities of acts, which can be perceived by the mature and sensitive moral consciousness. We say that a man's act is the whole difference he makes, and that this is right when it is the best possible.

213. DISCRETION

Now, to me it seems clear that what our Lord has done for us is to lay down certain principles for application which are themselves expressive of a spirit in which we are to live, but that He always leaves to us the question how those principles are in fact to be applied.

214. MORAL DEPRAVITY

When a being capable of spiritual discrimination blindly obeys an appetite, this is not, as moral conduct, identical with obedience to the same appetite on the part of an animal which has no power of spiritual discrimination. In the animal it is natural, even when to human taste it is distressing; in the man it is evidence of defect when it is not proof of depravity.

March Twelfth

215. HUMAN PROBLEMS

Man is both animal and spiritual. On one side he is the most fully developed of the animals; but if that were all, he would present, and know, no problems.

216. SPIRITUAL ARROGANCE

That an individual, who is called to the august responsibility of determining his own response to what he accepts as in some sense at least the self-revelation of God, should fail to make use of the best help that he can find, would be wanton arrogance. . . . He will think it most unlikely that he should be right and the common testimony of the saints be wrong.

217. INTELLECTUAL DIFFICULTIES

How often does the weak will obscure the clear call of conscience by resort to intellectual "difficulties"! Some of these are real enough; but some are sheer self-protection against the exacting claim of the holy love of God.

March Thirteenth

218. RIGHTS OF MAN

There can be no Rights of Man except on the basis of faith in God. But if God is real, and all men are His sons, that is the true worth of every one of them. My worth is what I am worth to God; and that is a marvellous great deal, for Christ died for me.

219. ADORING COMPANIONSHIP

He will draw to Himself *all men*—even Caiaphas and Pilate, even Judas;—even me, at last, not only (as already, I trust) to a genuine though intermittent devotion, a deliberate though half-hearted service, but to that fullness of adoring companionship which is foreshadowed in the promise *where I am* in the intimate fellowship of the Father's love, *there also shall my servant be*.

220. WRATH OF GOD

If "anger" and "wrath" are taken to mean the emotional reaction of an irritated self-concern, there is no such thing in God. But if God is holy love, and I am in any degree given to uncleanness or selfishness, then there is, in that degree, stark antagonism in God against me.

March Fourteenth

221. TAKING THE CROSS

What was universally expected of the Messiah was that He should found the Kingdom of God; one of the most familiar images was that of a triumphal procession which He would lead, and He warns them what it would be like. There is going to be a triumphal procession, He says, but it will not look like one. What it will look like is a gang of condemned criminals following their Leader to a place of execution. "If any man would come after Me, let him take up his cross and follow Me."

222. INVITATION TO VICTORY

Christ is winning; and He asks us to join His victorious host as members of His Army. The terms of the invitation are familiar; If any man will come after Me, let him deny himself (not think about himself in this world or any other world) and take up his cross (be ready for just anything) and follow Me.

223. ATROPHIED POWERS
Our fellowship with Christ not only hallows and intensifies all the powers that we have when we first meet with Him. It restores those which are atrophied by neglect or abuse. It is part of the deadly quality of sin that it hinders us from seeking its cure.

March Fifteenth

224. TRUST
Trust, which is always on the way to being love, must be spontaneous or non-existent. It grows of itself within our hearts as we come to appreciate the character and wisdom of someone whose record we know; and it grows most surely when we come to know personally in actual companionship someone who, the more we know him, inspires in us more trust and confidence in his character and wisdom.

225. JUDGMENT SELF-IMPOSED
St. John sets before us the story of the Lord's life as a process of judgment wherein are distinguished those who can and those who cannot perceive what is before them. For "the Jews," as he always speaks of them, heard most of the words and saw most of the acts which the disciples also heard and saw, but they did not behold His glory.

226. PERSONALITY AND GOD
The notion of personality as a definite idea first developed among Christians in their thought of God, not in their thought of man; it is historically not true that men first reached the whole idea of personality in themselves and then imagined God was like themselves. The whole history of philosophy proves the contrary. . . . Because man has in some degree a real share in the divine life, they began to think of him as a person.

March Sixteenth

227. EFFECT OF SOCIAL ENVIRONMENT

More potent than school or even than home, as a moral influence, is the whole structure of society, and especially its economic structure. This fixes for all their place in the general scheme; and the way in which they gain and keep that place of necessity determines a great deal of their conduct and profoundly influences their outlook upon life.

228. MENTAL GROWTH

The mind grows always by intercourse with a mind more mature than itself. That is the secret of all teaching.

229. EXAMINATION

One of the fundamental facts about education which is constantly ignored, is that the examiners are precisely as idle as the examinees, and that they therefore tend to conduct the examination in the way which saves them trouble, or at any rate to avoid conducting it in a way which would increase their trouble.

March Seventeenth

230. INCARNATION, BEFORE AND AFTER

These, then, are the marks of a true revelation; a union of holiness and power, before which our spirits bow in awe, and which authenticates itself by continuous development to some focal point in which all preparatory revelation finds fulfilment, and from which illumination radiates into every department of life and being.

231. INCARNATION—A REVELATION OF A CHANGELESS GOD

It is not incidental to God's eternity that (if the Christian Gospel be true) He lived and suffered and triumphed in the process of time. If that happened, then His eternal being is such as to necessitate its happening, so that its not happening would prove His eternal being to be other than Christianity believes. The quality of God's eternal life is such that "it behoved the Christ to suffer."

232. GLORY OF GOD

While the events make no difference in the quality of love which is expressed in them, yet the activity of the expression is a part of the fullness of the eternal love. Thus we may truly say that the glory of God is not only revealed in, but actually in part consists in, the death and Resurrection of Christ.

March Eighteenth

233. FULL CONSCIENCE

By "conscience" I mean the individual's conviction concerning right and wrong. Sometimes it is a reflective judgment, sometimes an emotional reaction, sometimes an intuitive perception. At its best it combines all three.

234. GOSPEL AND GREEK ETHICS

Plato never took the step from Justice to Love in his conception of the Idea of Good. This is the point—the vital point—at which the ethics of the Gospel leave the ethics of Greek philosophy far behind.

235. APPLYING PRINCIPLES

I hold that Christians are responsible for endeavouring to apply the principles of their faith to the actual problems of life, regarding them not as a source of direct instructions, but as an indication of the goal to be aimed at and as a standard of judgment to which policy must be referred.

March Nineteenth

236. WAR AND TRUTH

War poisons the wells of truth and strangles the mutual confidence of peoples hardly less in the times of peace than when fighting is actually going on. The possibility of it is a blight upon the fairest flowers of true civilisation.

237. WARTIME CONTROLS

The controls over private enterprise, established for war-time purposes, shall be retained when peace returns. They will, of course, call for modification; but they must not be abolished.

238. Agreement on Tariffs

It seems to me indispensable that States should consent to submit their Tariffs to the League and let free consultation concerning them take place. To impose a tariff without submitting it should be an offence within the competence of the Court of International Justice.

March Twentieth

239. Solving Problems

There is no Christian solution of the problems presented by human self-will; but there is a Christian cure for the self-will, and if that is effective, the problem is (not solved but) abolished.

240. Letter and Spirit

People sometimes say, when they are excusing themselves for a departure from some rule, that they do not govern their lives by the letter but by the spirit. What they mean, of course, is that they break their rules whenever they feel inclined. But the spirit is going to be much more exacting than the letter.

241. Rest and Idleness

What is the ultimate ground of the sabbath-law? It is, as the text of the Fourth Commandment makes clear, that God rested on the seventh day from the activity of Creation. . . . But the Lord repudiates the thought that the divine rest from Creation took the form of idleness: "My Father worketh even until now."

March Twenty-first

242. Limitation of Knowledge

God Himself, so far as His experience is temporal, has not absolute knowledge when the response that gives Him full sovereignty will be made; so that it is said "Of that day and of that hour knoweth no man, neither the Son" who is the divine Word, God self-manifested in the created process.

243. Sphere of Revelation

We find revelation at its highest where God finds occasion for unusual action, and we find it then both in the choice of occasion for such unusual action (for the divine character is revealed in its estimate of such and such an occasion as sufficient) and in the mode of action taken.

244. OMNIPOTENCE

When that purpose of God would be itself defeated by some anticipated occurrence, that occurrence is in fact impossible— as Christ suggested when he met the alarm of His disciples with the implication that the boat which carried the hope of the world could not sink.

March Twenty-second

245. VOCATIONAL GUIDANCE

The principle of divine vocation . . . relieves the moral philosopher from every claim that he should so articulate the conception of moral good as to provide clear guidance for individual action.

246. THE CALL TO THE MINISTRY

But if you are in doubt how you may best lay out your life, and if you are quite clear in your acceptance of Jesus Christ as your Saviour and your God, then the mere circumstances of the time constitute a call to the Church's direct service in its ministry which you must face; for there is no sphere of life in which a man can more certainly lay out all his talents in the service of God. It will call for every capacity; it will bring you into touch with human beings in every conceivable relation. There is no life so rich or so full of all those joys which come from serving people at the point of their greatest need.

247. CHRISTIAN ALTERNATION

There are men who are brought to God through their effort to serve their neighbours. There are men who are inspired to serve their neighbours by their fellowship with God. But the two cannot be separated, and if either appears to be existing without the other there is something wrong in it.

March Twenty-third

248. HISTORIC FOUNDATIONS OF CHRISTIANITY

Christianity is not primarily a system of ideas divinely communicated, nor a way of life divinely enjoined or guided, nor a method of worship divinely taught. It is primarily a self-revelation of God in a historical Person, and in that Person's life, death and resurrection.

249. BAD RELIGION

Religion itself, when developed to real maturity, knows quite well that the first object of its condemnation is bad Religion, which is a totally different thing from irreligion, and can be a very much worse thing.

250. REINCARNATION

It is not so widely recognised that the doctrine of Kharma is essentially materialistic. But it is hard to acquit of that charge a doctrine which attributes continuity of moral being, and liability to the penal consequences of acts done in a former existence, to a soul-substance which has no persistent self-consciousness.

March Twenty-fourth

251. VINDICTIVENESS IN IDEAS OF GOD

In the long run, punishment which is unending is plainly retributive only ; it may have a deterrent use while this life lasts, but from the Day of Judgment onwards it would lose that quality; and it obviously has no reformative aim. Now it requires much ingenuity to save from the charge of vindictiveness a character which inflicts forever a punishment which can be no other than retributive.

252. EVERLASTING SELF-CENTREDNESS

For the self-centred spirit there can be no eternal life. Even if it should exist for ever, its existence could only be an ever deepening chill of death. Because it seeks its satisfaction in itself, where none is to be found, it must suffer an always intenser pang of spiritual hunger, which cannot be allayed until that spirit turns to another source of satisfaction. In the self which it contemplates there can only be successive states. The self is not sufficient to inspire a dedication such as brings purposive unity into life.

253. A Shrinking Soul

The self-centred or self-concerned soul, making itself the object of its contemplation, and seeing all else as related to itself, is trying to feed upon itself. The food may be congenial, but the process is inevitably one of wastage. Such a soul must shrink and shrivel, suffering at last both the pain of unsatisfied hunger and the pain of contraction.

March Twenty-fifth

254. Spiritual Detachment

To live in the world yet in spiritual detachment from the world, is a harder moral task than to seek isolation from the world in voluntary poverty.

255. Cleric and Layman

The layman finds in religion the strength for doing in a Christian spirit work which unbelievers also do. The priest's work is religion. . . . Hence he lays upon devotional observance a stress which seems to many laymen disproportionate. . . . One of our chief needs is a clear recognition of the proper difference between the religion of the layman and of the cleric. Then we may reach the point where the priest will stand for the things of God before the laity—who seek the help that a religious specialist can give them, while the laity stand for the things of God before the world.

256. Church's Concern for Justice

I am convinced that one reason why the Church has counted for comparatively little in the public affairs of recent times is that its spokesmen have talked a great deal too much about love and not nearly enough about justice.

March Twenty-sixth

257. Proclaiming the Gospel

There is the temptation felt by religious teachers to substitute the argumentative introduction to religion for the authoritative proclamation of the Gospel as the good news given by God concerning Himself.

258. COMMUNISM

The great and profound difference between Christian civilisation and the kind of civilisation which the Communists are aiming at lies in our affirmation that the primary fact of the world is God, that each individual man is the child of God, that at the root of his being he is as a child of God, and that he is a child of God before he is a citizen of any national community. . . . If you cut out the religious and spiritual background of human nature, then I do not think there is any direct answer to the Communistic philosophy or any ground of real resistance to it.

259. ASTRONOMY AND PARISH CHURCH

There ought to be no sense of either discord or irrelevance between the teaching in the Parish Church and the impact of astronomy upon the imagination.

March Twenty-seventh

260. SURVIVAL OF DEATH NECESSARY

It is not reasonable that if a man lives like a devil he should be permitted to die like a dog. Survival of physical death would be required if only to ensure that spiritual death were other than merely animal decease.

261. EXPERIENCING DEATH

The Lord does not promise that anyone who keeps His word shall avoid the physical incident called death; but that if his mind is turned towards that word it will not pay any attention to death; death will be to it irrelevant. It may truly be said that such a man will not "experience" death, because, though it will happen to him, it will matter to him no more than the fall of a leaf from a tree under which he might be reading a book.

262. DUTY AND REWARD

Follow me: that is the whole of a Christian's duty. *And where I am there also shall my servant be:* that is the whole of a Christian's reward.

March Twenty-eighth

263. RESOLVING PROBLEMS

There are many superficial problems which can be resolved only by making them profound problems.

264. LIVING FOR A CAUSE

It is easier to die for a cause than to live for it; living for it means the setting aside of pleasure and self-interest in a host of little choices, where there is no glory, at least in men's eyes, on the one side, and no open shame on the other.

265. CHRISTIANITY FRIGHTENING

If Christianity has never frightened us, we have not yet learnt what it is.

March Twenty-ninth

266. DECADENCE

It is a signal mark of decadence when people are more troubled by pain than by sin, by suffering than by moral evil.

267. ORIGIN OF SOCIAL EVILS

The great evils of society do not result from the startling and appalling wickedness of some few individuals; they are the result of a few million people like ourselves living together; and if anyone wants to see the picture of his sin, let him look at slums, and wars, and the like. These things have their origin in characters like ours, ready, no doubt, to be generous with superfluities, but in the last resort self-centred, with alike the defensiveness and aggressiveness that go with that self-centredness.

268. GOD AND EVIL

It is not permissible for any Christian to say that anything that God made is inherently evil. Incidentally, when St. John wanted to make his great proclamation he did not say, "The Word became man"; he deliberately took the word which represents the lowest elements in human' nature and said, "The Word became flesh."

March Thirtieth

269. INSIGHT OF SYMPATHY

"Thou shalt love thy neighbour as thyself." But love is not at our command. We may force ourselves to act as if we loved, but it can only be with partial success; for where real love is absent there is failure also of the insight of sympathy by which the true welfare of the neighbour is discerned. Conscientiousness without love is clumsy.

270. LOVING ENEMIES

Anyone can love his friends; anyone can love people who are kind to him; the test is "Love your enemies." That is forgiveness. Treat your enemies as if they were your friends. That is the great test of whether your heart is in tune with God; for that is what God Himself does. He sends His rain on the just and the unjust, and we are to be perfect in the same way that our Heavenly Father is perfect—that is, with the perfection of indiscriminating love.

271. THE LOVING ATHEIST

We shall say without hesitation that the atheist who is moved by love is moved by the spirit of God; an atheist who lives by love is saved by his faith in the God whose existence (under that name) he denies.

March Thirty-first

272. SELFISH PRAYER

If your prayer is selfish, the answer will be something that will rebuke your selfishness. You may not recognise it as having come at all, but it is sure to be there.

273. ANSWER TO PRAYER

For it is a law of the spiritual life from which there is no escape, that we receive in proportion to what we give—much more than we give, thank God, or we should be in a sorry plight, but still in proportion.

274. THE SHAPING OF CHARACTER

Our characters are shaped by our companions and by the objects to which we give most of our thoughts and with which we fill our imaginations. We cannot always be thinking even about Christ, but we can refuse to dwell on any thoughts which are out of tune with Him. We can, above all, quite deliberately turn our minds towards Him at any time when those thoughts come in.

APRIL

April First

275. RIGHT HAND OF GOD

The Flesh and Blood of the Ascended Son of Man are plainly not mere matter; if they were, the resultant astronomical problems would be overwhelming—for where in the universe are they? "By the right hand of the Father" where the Ascended Son is seated is not a far-off place; it is here; wherever a man be, for him it is here. The Flesh and Blood of the Ascended Son of Man are Spirit and Life.

276. FASTING COMMUNION

It is appropriate to recall how recent is any widespread concern in the Church of England about this requirement of fasting. Archbishop Davidson once told me that he knew it for a fact that Mr. Keble all his days paid no observance to any such rule. In the mediæval Church, when no doubt the rule obtained, Communion was rare; if our aim is to encourage frequent Communion, we must be very careful how we impose in England a rule quite easy to observe in Italy.

277. ACTS OF REVERENCE

Why should not my body, which is the symbol and organ of my spirit, make a bodily gesture symbolic of spiritual reverence before those material objects which have been consecrated to be the symbols and vehicles of Christ's spiritual self-giving?

April Second

278. PSYCHOLOGY AND LOGIC

Because Psychology studies mental processes, it is very liable to behave as if Logic (the study of the validity of mental processes) were one of its own subdivisions. But in fact Psychology, like every other science, must pre-suppose the autonomy of Logic; otherwise the writings of psychologists could be no more than their own autobiographies.

279. Limitation of "Natural Theology"

If the Natural Theologian is to know in any real sense the subject-matter of his study, he must know it from within by personal experience; that is, he must know it as a worshipper. Otherwise he will resemble a blind man who writes criticisms of the Royal Academy's Exhibition.

280. Petitio Principii

If you begin by attending to objects only in so far as they are measurable, you are likely to end by having only their measurements before your attention.

April Third

281. Sanctification

The Holy Spirit, as Christians know Him, is not merely the diffused power of God discoverable everywhere in the universe, but is first and foremost the special and distinctive influence which God exerts over our souls as we respond to His love in the human life of Christ. And the difference is fundamentally this; that now, instead of having regulations which we are to obey, deliberately considering how they apply, we have, in the degree in which we dwell in Christ's companionship, a desire to do the things that please God.

282. Co-operation with Non-Christians

There is no difficulty in finding the movements of the Spirit, because wherever the fruits of the Spirit are, there is He. If you find something going forward which promotes true fellowship, there you know the Holy Spirit is at work, and you may come yourself increasingly under His influence by taking your share there. It may be that those with whom you join are not themselves Christians, and do not recognise the power that is moving them for what it is. Never mind that. You may have the opportunity of helping them to understand it, to their inestimable gain. But if you cannot, do not let that hinder your co-operation; for it still is the work of the Holy Spirit.

283. The Divine Spirit

Always the breath—the wind—of the Spirit is moving. We know it by its effect. We have no need to ask for its authentication—Is it Protestant? Is it Catholic? Where the fruit of the Spirit is apparent, there the Spirit is at work. We should place ourselves in its course that we may be carried by its impulse, even though this leads us to association with strange comrades.

April Fourth

284. EUCHARISTIC OBLATION

One main element in Eucharistic worship is our incorporation into the One Body in which Christ makes His eternal self-oblation to the Father.

285. EUCHARISTIC RECEPTION

No doubt it is true that the Bread and Wine are after Consecration the Flesh and Blood of the Son of Man. But there is danger that we may turn that objective truth into a subjective delusion by supposing that to receive by the mouth the consecrated species is to receive eternal life. Therefore we must be reminded that the flesh doth not profit at all, if it be only flesh, and even though it be the flesh of the Son of Man.

286. INTERCOMMUNION LIMITED

There are countless ways of expressing a spiritual unity which falls short of demanding organic union; we must not give away for this purpose the only means we have for expressing and realising organic union itself.

April Fifth

287. TRUE WORSHIP

This alone is true worship—the giving to God of body, soul and spirit ("ourselves, our souls and bodies") with all that they need for their full development, so that He may take and use them for His purpose.

288. VISION OF GOD

If a man should claim to have had a vision of God which did not bring him to penitence, I should feel very sure either that he had had no real vision, or that it was not a vision of the real God.

289. MOULDING INFLUENCES
Whatever the freedom of the will may mean, it is sheer nonsense if it means that a selfish man can make himself unselfish. What, then, can you do about it? You can make what is far the most important choice anybody ever has to make at all; that is the choice of those influences by which you deliberately submit yourself to be moulded. You can, in your better moments, determine that there shall no day pass in which you do not spend so much time in deliberate contemplation of Jesus Christ, and in the desire to be made like Him so far as you are able to feel the desire.

April Sixth

290. PARTNERSHIP
Each wants to be a good Pharisee, or a good Sadducee—a good Catholic or a good Evangelical. Instead of penetrating to the living heart of the tradition, which was God-given, each eyes his neighbour, and seeks his applause. So partisans are made, for whom faith itself is perverted.

291. MORAL PARADOXES
One of the commonest of the compromises that have been made is for the world to allow the Church to be at peace in proclaiming what may be called its philosophical paradoxes provided that it keeps quiet about its moral ones.

292. DISESTABLISHMENT
Disestablishment is, properly speaking, of no interest to the Church. It is entirely a question for the State to determine whether or not it should associate itself with the Divine Society. If it wishes to do so, on terms which do not hamper the Church in the discharge of its own mission, this recognition by the State of the Sovereignty of God is naturally welcomed by the Church. But the concern of the Church must be the retention of its freedom to fulfil its own commission.

April Seventh

293. GOD CONVEYED IN SACRAMENT

A sacrament is something more than a divine poem, because it conveys not only God's meaning to the mind, but God Himself to the whole person of the worshipper.

294. SACRAMENTS OF THE CHURCH

Christ now acts in the world through His Body the Church. All particular Sacraments belong to the Church, and have their meaning within its corporate life. If we are to understand them, we must consider their place in the corporate life of the Christian society and proceed from this to their value for the individual. To invert this process and ask first (for example) what is the spiritual difference between a baptised infant and an unbaptised, is to confuse the problem in advance.

295. SACRAMENTAL ACCESSIBILITY

All things are present to Him, and are what they are by His creative will. In and through all of them He is accessible; there is therefore no contradiction in the supposition that in and through certain physical elements, by methods which He has chosen because of their appropriateness to our psycho-physical nature, He renders Himself in a peculiar degree accessible to those who seek Him through such media.

April Eighth

296. MAN'S PART IN REDEMPTION

All is of God; the only thing of my very own which I can contribute to my own redemption is the sin from which I need to be redeemed.

297. THE ONLY TRUE GOOD

It may be bad for the sinner to know that God is going to save him, unless he has at least some present experience of the process of that salvation; but it is supremely good for the sinner to know as a fact of his own experience that God has saved him—indeed that is, in the last resort, the only good for him that there is.

298. SPIRITUAL REDEMPTION

What is quite certain is that the self cannot by any effort of its own lift itself off its own self as centre and resystematise itself about

God as its centre. Such radical conversion must be the act of God, and that too by some process other than the gradual self-purification of a self-centred soul assisted by the ever-present influence of God diffused through nature, including human nature. It cannot be a process only of enlightenment. Nothing can suffice but a redemptive act. Something impinging upon the self from without must deliver it from the freedom which is perfect bondage to the bondage which is its only perfect freedom.

April Ninth

299. MIND AND SPIRIT
When mind becomes active not only in choosing means to ends, but in choosing between ends, it is rightly called Spirit.

300. NATURE AND MIND
The more deeply mind is seen to be rooted in nature—in matter if you like—the more manifestly is it impossible to account for nature or matter in any other terms than those of mind.

301. SPIRITUAL ENERGY
The one self-explanatory fact is the full energy of spiritual life active in the achievement of the good.

April Tenth

302. MORAL OBTUSENESS
Always remember, when you experiment with your soul, that you can never judge the result. No crime looks so bad to the man who has committed it as to the man who has kept clear of it. As soon as we have done something that is nasty, we have blunted our own capacity to be disgusted, we have tarnished the mirror in which we are to look at our own reflection.

303. MORAL EDUCATION
The call of conscientiousness is a call to make the hero's stake of his life on what seems to him best though he can prove it to be so only by the hazard that he makes. The moral life is an adventure not only in detail but in principle.

304. SIN IS IRRATIONAL

We know it is morally wrong, and we know it is self-destructive, yet rather than pluck out our right eye, rather even than close it, we fling our whole body into hell. It is no use trying to find reasons for doing this; reason is all on the other side, as we know quite well when we act. We do not even think the present good greater than the more remote. We do not think at all. We just say, "Here goes!"

April Eleventh

305. PROGRESS AND ORIGINALITY

The modern world with its strange, new and probably transient belief in "progress," tends to give much credit to "originality," even to the point of doubting whether anything else is quite sincere. . . . Where the eternal truths are concerned the search for originality by speaker or hearer is a puerility.

306. GOSPEL AND SCIENCE

The Gospel is no more established because Sir James Jeans finds the universe more like a thought than like a machine, than it is imperilled when Sir Arthur Keith finds no grounds for belief in immortality.

307. TELLING THE TRUTH

There is always a *prima facie* obligation to tell the truth. But there are some circumstances in which we recognise that it is not only permissible, but obligatory, to say what is false. The stock instance, of course, is that of the murderer asking which way his victim has gone.

April Twelfth

308. FREEDOM OF CHILD OF GOD

If I claim freedom over against the State because I am a child of God and must obey Him rather than men, there is no risk (except so far as I delude myself) that I shall use this freedom to pursue my own advantage to the detriment of either my neighbour or society as a whole.

309. Freedom with Control

Is there anything known in the world which does control conduct by means of and not by over-riding freedom? Yes; one thing only—the sacrifice of love.

310. Free Will and Determination by Love

There is one condition on which our conduct can be both free and externally determined. It is found wherever a man acts in a certain way in order to give pleasure to one whom he loves. Such acts are free in the fullest degree; yet their content is wholly determined by the pleasure of the person loved.

April Thirteenth

311. Patriotism

The Englishman should be loyal to England, not because it is his country, but because he is its citizen—not because in some sense it belongs to him, but because in a far deeper sense he belongs to it.

312. Nationality

The duty of an Englishman to a Frenchman is not to treat him as if he were an Englishman, or as if no national distinctions existed, but to recognise that devotion to France is as excellent in him as love of England is in an Englishman.

313. National and Individual Morality

You often hear it said, what is morally wrong cannot be politically right. What people mean when they say it is usually that no nation, for example, ought to treat another nation in a different way from that in which one individual ought to treat another. I am sure that is not true.

April Fourteenth

314. Affirmation of Community

When a man for duty's sake sacrifices his own interest or his life, he affirms himself in his capacity of membership to be more and better than his isolated self with all its pleasures and pains.

315. Forming Public Opinion

If we only had the common pluck to speak instead of remaining in silence with a silly smirk on our faces when things are said which let the standard down! When the stand is made, we find that most people about us are very glad it has been made; but it needs courage for one to take the lead.

316. Imperialism

A British citizen will not be less glad of the British Empire because of his Christianity; but this will make him careful to attach his joy to its record of justice, freedom, and trustworthiness, not to its mere extent or the capacity of British people to impose their will on others.

April Fifteenth

317. The Church and Relativities of History

This does not mean that in the actual world no one course of action is right; it means that the right course is to be found by striking a balance of goods and evils, and will be found to involve the forgoing of some goods, probably also the acceptance of some evils. The Church, in its historical situation and in its actual decisions, is bound to the relativities of all historical action as completely as anyone or anything else.

318. Character Training

It is quite possible for character to improve under the pressure of disciplinary sanctions, and for self-regard to be partly undermined by appeal to self-regarding motives.

319. Christian Prejudice

The Christian, who goes into the world full of love and trust, will find that experience confirms his "prejudice," for to him men will show the finer and more sensitive sides of their nature, and even where there was no generosity his love and trust will, at least sometimes, create it.

April Sixteenth

320. EVOLUTION AND PROGRESS

It is always worth while to inquire how far the doctrine of evolution has anything to do with any reasonable notion of progress. . . . If you take an unarmed saint and confront him with a hungry tiger, there will be a struggle for existence culminating in the survival of the fittest, which means, of course, the fittest to survive in those conditions; but it will not be a survival of the ethically best. There is no reason to suppose that the struggle for existence always favours what is ethically admirable.

321. THE FALL OF MAN

Over and over again, as we break some rule which seems rather arbitrary and meaningless, we discover the principle which had dictated it. We set in motion the causes and effects from which we understand, for the first time, why there had ever been that prohibition; then it is too late. The discovery is called the Fall of Man.

322. HOLY SPIRIT AND OBLIGATION

In the science of ethics, the sense of obligation—the sense that there are some things which, if the opportunity comes, we must do, and that there are certain other things which, whatever the advantage to be derived from them, we must on no account do—this is the Holy Spirit.

April Seventeenth

323. EUCHARISTIC SELF-OBLATION

What Christ has done for us only avails for us so far as through the surrender of our wills to Him He also does it in us. We must not come before the Father offering Him as our sin-offering and not offering ourselves.

324. BROKEN BODY

As His fleshly Body was then to be broken in correspondence to the symbol which expressed the spiritual sacrifice and interpreted its consummation on Calvary, so now it is that Body which we constitute that is to be broken, and in our wills and lives that the sacrifice is to be dedicated and consummated.

325. COMMUNISM AND FEAR

You cannot make people unselfish by the application of fear. The only way to make people unselfish is through the appeal of love to their hearts; to attempt by terror to make men abandon selfishness is useless. The Communist discipline of fear can never do the one thing that Communists desire to bring about.

April Eighteenth

326. MAN'S CHIEF END

The proper object of the self's surrender is the Spirit of the Whole which we call God; but if attention is diverted from God Himself to the self's satisfaction in being surrendered to Him, adoration itself is poisoned. The satisfaction is real, and there is no reason for refraining from attention to it so long as it is in the second place. Man's chief end is to glorify God and (incidentally) to enjoy Him for ever.

327. MAN IS GOD'S AGENT

God calls us to yield ourselves—our souls and bodies—a living sacrifice to Him, that through us by the Holy Spirit He may do His own work. Because He loves us, we must believe that our refusal grieves Him: but His mighty purpose does not depend on our paltry contribution.

328. STRENGTH OF THE CHRISTIAN

To the man who has heard God's call the chief source of strength is in the recollection that the Divine Majesty is not dependent on his strength, his wisdom, or even his fidelity.

April Nineteenth

329. GRACE: THE LOVE OF GOD

Grace is not something other than God, imparted by Him; it is the very Love of God (which is Himself) approaching and seeking entry to the soul of man.

330. MEDITATION

Our duty is not primarily to strive and to brace up our wills; but primarily to fasten our attention upon the divine love, that it may do its own work upon us and within us.

331. CHRIST'S COMPASSION
Jesus *found him.* The man did not find Jesus; Jesus found him. That is the deepest truth of Christian faith; Jesus found me. Our fellowship with Him is rooted in His compassion.

April Twentieth

332. FEAR AND LOVE
The loving God is holy, and we are both selfish and unclean. "Perfect love casteth out fear," but none will dare to say his love is perfect. And whatsoever in us is still selfish must fear not only with awe but with terror. For it must perish from before the Face of God; it must be burnt up in the consuming fire of His holy love.

333. PURGATORY
Hell has in effect been banished from popular belief; and as Purgatory had been banished long before, we are left with a very widespread sentimental notion that all persons who die are forthwith in Paradise or Heaven. And this seems to involve a conception of God as so genially tolerant as to be morally indifferent, and converts the belief in immortality from a moral stimulant to a moral narcotic.

334. SELF-REGARDING FEAR
It is probably good for most people to have an occasional shock of fright with reference to their shortcomings; but there is no doubt that to live under the constant pressure of fear—in the sense of anxiety concerning one's self—is deeply demoralising.

April Twenty-first

335. EUCHARISTIC SACRIFICE—SPIRITUAL ACT
The spiritual act of sacrifice took place when Judas passed out under the Lord's protecting silence, and the Lord took the Bread which He called His Body and broke and gave it. Then was made the sacrifice of will, the essential sacrifice.

336. BLOOD OF CHRIST
The reason why the Jews were forbidden to eat the blood of their sacrifices is itself the reason why we must drink the blood of the

Son of Man. The blood is the life; especially is it the life released by death that it may be offered to God.

337. FASTING COMMUNION
It is perfectly legitimate to commend this practice as a sign of reverence for the sacrament and an expression of fellowship with the greater part of the Church; it is not legitimate, in the Church of England, where it clearly fell into desuetude, to require it as of obligation.

April Twenty-second

338. FAITH AND DOCTRINE
Faith is not the holding of correct doctrines, but personal fellowship with the living God. Correct doctrine will both express this, assist it and issue from it; incorrect doctrine will misrepresent this and hinder or prevent it. I do not believe in any creed, but I use certain creeds to express, to conserve, and to deepen my belief in God. What is offered to man's apprehension in any specific Revelation is not truth concerning God but the living God Himself.

339. FAITH—A STARTING POINT
The central and basic element in Christianity is not a doctrine about God, but is God Himself active in the Incarnate Lord. Faith is not a conclusion but a starting-point; reasoning will enrich its content, but that new content when incorporated into the apprehension of Faith becomes a fresh starting-point for thought and practice.

340. LOVE AND KNOWLEDGE
Real and complete knowledge in persons of other persons is not distinguishable from love ; it is not so much that the two go together as that the two words express two aspects of one thing. To understand a person means rather to sympathise with him than to have a scientific apprehension of his motives, temperament and character. When understanding is perfected in knowledge properly so called, sympathy is perfected in love.

April Twenty-third

341. SENSE OF OBLIGATION

The sense of obligation is the spontaneous reaction of a person who is a member of society towards acts or suggestions which conform to or contradict the standards of conduct which under the influence of experience have come to be accepted in his community.

342. A COMMON DELUSION

Our countrymen have a rooted tendency to believe that the distinction between right and wrong is not only absolute in principle but evident in fact. This is a complete delusion, and a source of much moral blindness.

343. LOYALTY TO A PERSON

We have no code of rules that can only be obeyed in the circumstances of their origin, no scheme of thought which can only be understood in the terms in which it was first conceived, but a Person to whom we can be loyal in all circumstances whatever, with that infinite flexibility and delicacy of adjustment which are compatible with a loyalty that remains absolute and unalterable.

April Twenty-fourth

344. THE UNIQUENESS OF CHRISTIANITY

Remember that Christianity is not just another religion of individual salvation, differing only in having a different plan of salvation to offer. It is the one and only religion of world-redemption. We are members of the family of God; when we come to Him in Christ, it must always be in the company of our brothers and sisters.

345. SALVATION IN COMMUNITY

The Biblical picture of salvation through incorporation into a community entrusted with the knowledge of divine truth fits closely with the modern understanding of mankind.

346. GOD'S ACTIVITY

"Blessed be the Lord God of Israel"—it is not a universally diffused essence of which we speak, but the Living God—"*for He hath visited and redeemed His People.*"

April Twenty-fifth

347. INDIFFERENCE

Of the forms of self-will, complete indifference to other people is the worst. Hatred at least recognises the other person as being of importance, and in essence, as well as by our psychological tendencies, is nearer to the moral relation with its culmination in love than is indifference.

348. SELFISH CONTAGION

The existence of one self-centred soul would spread an evil infection through all who come within its range of influence. This happens both positively by suggestion and negatively by repulsion. If A is self-centred, B tends to become so by imitation; but also B becomes so in self-defence. The instincts of gregariousness and of fear combine to produce the same result.

349. THE ROOT OF SIN

None of the purely evolutionary theories of sin touches the centre of the problem, for no man who is really conscious of sin will be content to have that consciousness explained as merely an indication that his growth is as yet incomplete. . . . It is not simply that he sees before him a goal he has not yet reached, but that he has seen a goal before him and has turned his back upon it.

April Twenty-sixth

350. THE OTHERNESS OF GOD

In so far as God and man are spiritual they are of one kind; in so far as God and man are rational, they are of one kind. But in so far as God creates, redeemed and sanctifies while man is created, redeemed and sanctified, they are of two kinds. God is not creature; man is not creator. God is not redeemed sinner, man is not redeemer from sin. At this point the Otherness is complete.

351. GOD'S GRACE

If we do not trust, it is because we cannot trust; any effort to have faith will convert faith itself into a "work of the law," and destroy its real character. For my salvation must be altogether His gift, and in no sense at all my achievement. And there are some who are not—at present, anyhow—able to receive it.

352. The Paradox of Grace

St. Paul undoubtedly argued that human sin was a special opportunity for divine Grace. Those who had no experience of that Grace drew the formally correct conclusion that we should "do evil that good may come." . . . The Apostle is content to retort upon its utterers the gloriously question-begging observation "whose damnation is just."

April Twenty-seventh

353. Real Freedom

The freedom that matters is not freedom to satisfy our momentary desires, but freedom to fulfil our steady and constant purpose. The main business of education is to strengthen our capacity to form and follow an adequate purpose throughout life.

354. Freedom basic to Christianity

Christianity, as is clear from the Gospels, stakes everything on human freedom. . . . The Gospels show Christ everywhere paying to the free personality of men and women a respect and trust which nothing—not even the intended treachery of Judas—could shake.

355. Freedom and Heredity

"Doing what I like" is what St. Paul accurately describes as "the body of this death"; for my likes and dislikes are not free; they are fixed by my heredity, training and circumstance.

April Twenty-eighth

356. Marriage in Church

I have for a considerable number of years held that we should gain rather than lose if the Church were to obtain release from obligation to do the State's business, and refused to solemnise the marriage of any who had not already been married in the eye of the law at the Registry Office, bestowing its blessing only on those who, as far as inquiry could disclose, mean by marriage what the Church means.

357. DIVORCE AND RE-MARRIAGE

The Church . . . should find some way at least, of bearing a quite unambiguous witness to the ideal with which it is entrusted, and for that reason, as it seems to me, the Church should decline ever to sanction the use of its own Marriage Service in the case of any person who has a partner to a former marriage still living, and this should, in my judgment, be applied quite equally to the so-called innocent and the so-called guilty party, partly because of the impossibility of truly assessing moral guilt in the matter.

358. EPISCOPAL GUIDANCE

It is not the business of an assembly of Bishops to declare that in certain circumstances specified sins may be committed.

April Twenty-ninth

359. THE REAL ENEMY

The real enemy to-day is not materialism; materialism as a philosophy is as dead as a doornail. The real enemy is a spiritual interpretation of the Universe which gives a place to the supreme values of the spiritual life—beauty, goodness and truth—but which does not give full value to the fact of Personality.

360. CONSECRATED DESIRE IS HOPE

Christian Hope is the consecration of desire, and desire is the hardest thing of all to consecrate. When you positively hope for the Kingdom of God, then your desire becomes consecrated. That will only happen as you begin to think how lovely the life according to Christ is.

361. THE WRATH OF GOD

That phrase "Kingdom of God" means primarily the Reign or Sovereignty of God; and there is evidently a most important sense in which that is a permanent and unalterable fact. We never escape from the Sovereignty of God; His law always operates. Yet in another sense His Sovereignty is incomplete so long as the operation of His law is manifest not in the obedience of His people but in the destruction which it brings upon the disobedient.

362. TRUTH AND BEAUTY OBLIGATORY

It is because a man's relation to Truth and Beauty is a social relation—a relation to another Mind or somewhat akin to Mind—that the claim of Truth and Beauty constitute an obligation, and not only the offer of an august satisfaction.

363. LOYALTY TO TRUTH

Now this loyalty to truth is inculcated in childhood as surely as faith in God, and there is a transition from the child's apprehension of it at second-hand to the scientist's independent grasp of it. But when he grasps it, it is not something which he masters; it is something which masters him.

364. LIMITATIONS OF ÆSTHETICS

Beethoven was a passionately conscientious artist, but he was not specially easy to live with. . . . Beauty drew the self from its self-centredness, but only in respect to certain functions. The deepest springs of life are not yet touched.

MAY

May First

365. LOVE AND THE UNIVERSE

To say that the controlling power of this vast Universe is Love, is to say something so infinite in its significance as to claim all the energies of life and thought in the exploration of it, so hyperbolically paradoxical as to call for the whole course of history for its verification.

366. GOD OTHER THAN LOVE

It is true that Majesty is not the only element in the Christian's conception of God. The very heart of the Christian Gospel is the proclamation that God is Love, but that proclamation is meaningless unless the word God initially stands for something other than Love. To say that Love is Love is to say nothing.

367. CHILDREN OF GOD

The writers of the New Testament all observe a certain use of language which has deep significance. They often imply that God is the Father of all men; but they do not speak of all men as His children; that expression is reserved for those who, by the grace of God, are enabled in some measure to reproduce His character.

May Second

368. IDEALISM

Idealism we regard as an error due to the effort to construct philosophy as a theory of cognition rather than as a theory of living experience.

369. NON-MEASURABLE ASPECTS OF REALITY

For even if it be admitted for the moment that the only world outside of consciousness is a world of measurables, yet these by their impact upon consciousness set up an experience of non-measurable qualities, and that experience with its content, being extant, is part of Ultimate Reality.

370. THE ESSENCE OF PERSONALITY

The essence of personality is intelligent choice or purpose. If you think out what makes the difference between a person and a thing, or a person and a brute, you cannot escape that conclusion. The billiard ball only goes where you push it. That is the most humiliating fact in my experience; but it is true. If I could only suppose it had a will of its own, I should be much happier.

May Third

371. WORKING FOR GOD: VOCATION

We never know who is doing the greatest work for God. Here is a man who holds great office in the Church and preaches to multitudes; yet at the end, all he has done is to keep things from falling back. And there is a girl, poor and uneducated, of whom no one ever thinks; but because she is loving and devout she sows the seed of life in a child entrusted to her care who grows up to be a missionary pioneer, or Christian statesman, or profound theologian—shaping the history of nations or the thought of generations.

372. FINDING VOCATION

The divine will or purpose, which determines my vocation, also determines all events or occurrences whatsoever, at least in the sense of fixing the order within which they take place. It must therefore be possible in principle for a man to discover his vocation by considering with sufficient thoroughness his own nature and his circumstances.

373. VOCATION AND VIRTUE

We must not forget that our vocation is so to practise virtue that men are won to it; it is possible to be morally upright repulsively.

May Fourth

374. THE EVER-ACTIVE WORD

The divine and creative Word was not uttered once for all, but it receives perpetual utterance in the radiation of light, in the movements of the stars, in the development of life, in the reason and conscience of man.

375. Inspiration

If Amos and Isaiah and the unknown author or authors of the Books of the Kings wrote "at the dictation of the Holy Ghost," then no doubt their content must be regarded as truth, but it is truth conveyed in a manner wholly without either parallel or analogy in the normal relationship between God and man, and even contradictory of that relationship.

376. The Conditions for Full Revelation

For two reasons the event in which the fullness of a revelation is given must be the life of a Person; the first is that the revelation is to persons who can fully understand only what is personal; the second is that the revelation is of a Personal Being.

May Fifth

377. Life and Worship

Worship includes all life and the moments spent in concentrated worship, whether "in Church" or elsewhere, are the focusing points of the sustaining and directing energy of the worshipper's whole life.

378. Achievement and Devotion

It is never the quantity of our achievement that is important, but always and only the quality of our devotion.

379. Fear of the Lord

Our response to that Gospel will be joyous, but also reverent. We shall run to our Father with cheerful cries, but we shall none the less approach the Eternal Majesty with trembling awe. His greatness and our littleness must always fill us with that feeling of insignificance and helplessness for which the only name is fear; and in that sense the fear of the Lord is not only the beginning of wisdom, but a permanent characteristic of all true religion.

May Sixth

380. Sacramental Communion

Sacramental communion is an end in itself so far as it is communion, but a means to an end so far as it is sacramental. The sacrament is normally necessary; but it is the communion alone that is vital.

381. Isolating Moments of Eucharist

So long as we abide by what is there in the Gospel story—the sacrifice or self-giving and the feeding on the Self so given—we know that we are true to His mind. When we isolate what He said as part of that action from the rest, especially when we draw inferences from a great dramatic utterance as if it were a proposition in a text-book, we can no longer be sure that we are true to His mind.

382. Relying on Sacramental Presence

Those who learn to rely on the help of Christ's sacramental Presence in their prayers may find it more difficult to apprehend His Presence when there is no sacramental medium at hand.

May Seventh

383. Pleasing God

He comes before us commanding still, but not only commanding—pleading. He asks not only for our obedience, but for our sympathy; what He wants above all things else is our affection—that our desire may be to do what will please Him. When we feel like that towards anyone on earth we call it loving him. We are to reach the point when we desire to do what pleases God for no reason beyond.

384. Winsome Attractiveness

All Christians have got to aim at being such people that our friends see in us a kind of life they would like to live, and of which they want to know the secret. You have got to exhibit the winsome attractiveness of Christ.

385. Christians in War

We are called to the hardest of all tasks; to fight without hatred, to resist without bitterness, and in the end, if God grant it so, to triumph without vindictiveness.

May Eighth

386. RELIGION FOR WHAT?

Some people say they do not need religion; do not need it for what? You do not need religion to make you as good as the world requires you to be; the help of the world itself is enough for that. You begin to feel the need of it when you have a vision of Christ as the standard for yourself and of the world as it might be, the world as it is in the mind of Christ.

387. WORSHIP AND DAILY DUTIES

All life ought to be worship; and we know quite well there is no chance it will be worship unless we have times when we have worship and nothing else. . . . Our duty to God requires that we should, for a good part of our time, be not consciously thinking about Him. That makes it absolutely necessary. . . that we should have our times which are worship, pure and simple.

388. RULES OF LIFE

You want rules . . . because if you leave yourself to drift, you always drift the wrong way. You do not drift into public worship; you do not drift into the service of Holy Communion. You let it go by, unless you make up your mind to use it; and you make your use of it comparatively futile unless you think out in advance how you will go, and what your preparation shall be.

May Ninth

389. REASON AND AUTHORITY

There is no contrast between Reason and Authority. It is impossible to accept a belief on Authority except so far as the Authority is accepted by Reason. In so far as a child's acceptance of what he is told is *totally* uncritical, that is not acceptance on Authority, but on the causal action of impressions received. His belief rests on Authority only when his acceptance of what he is told is due to *trust* in those who tell.

390. FUNCTION OF DOCTRINE

Doctrinal or credal formulæ had their importance as pointing to Him, by trust in whom His followers had found peace; they were not themselves the revelation, but signposts indicating where the revelation was to be found.

391. REVERENCE FOR "LAW"

No Law, apart from a Lawgiver, is a proper object of reverence. It is mere brute fact; and every living thing, still more every person exercising intelligent choice, is its superior. The reverence of persons can be appropriately given only to that which itself is at least personal.

May Tenth

392. NATURAL SELF-CENTREDNESS

The scientist who labours devotedly in the service of truth is sometimes very jealous about the credit for his discoveries; the artist who is true to his own ideal of beauty is not always generous in appreciation of other artists; the philanthropist who sacrifices ease and comfort in a life of service is sometimes extremely self-willed as regards the kind of service which he or she shall render. And any one of these may be an exacting member of the home circle.

393. ABIDING CONSEQUENCES OF SIN

If I allow myself to become set in self-centredness the love of God can only reach me through the pain that causes or results from the break-up of that self-centredness; and when it has found me, and stirred my penitence, and won me to forgiveness, I am still the forgiven sinner, not the always loyal child of God.

394. FREEDOM OF CONSCIENCE

Freedom of conscience—that is the sacred thing: not freedom to do what I choose or to fulfil my own purpose, but freedom to do what I ought, and to fulfil God's purpose for me.

May Eleventh

395. STATE AND PUNISHMENT

With wickedness as such the State has simply nothing to do. And if the State begins to base its penal action upon moral assessments, it finds itself involved in usurping the prerogatives of God and attempting to pronounce judgment where no man has the necessary knowledge.

396. CHRISTIAN CIVILISATION

What do we mean by a Christian civilisation? . . . We mean a civilisation in which the Christian standards of value are accepted as those by which both persons and policies are to be judged, and in which there is a steady effort to guide policy by Christian principles.

397. DEMOCRACY NOT FOR ALL

Not all peoples have been able to maintain order through democratic institutions; and unless they can, it is futile to say that a theological principle "demands" democracy.

May Twelfth

398. CALL TO SERVICE

The way to call anyone into fellowship with us is, not to offer them service, which is liable to arouse the resistance of their pride, but to ask service from them. Of course, the request must be prompted by a real need . . . So the Almighty God seeks to win us to fellowship with Himself by putting some part of His purpose into our hands.

399. THE INVITATION OF CHRIST

He never says, "If any man will come after Me, I will deliver him from the pains of hell and give him the joys of heaven." He calls men to take up their cross and share His sacrifice. To those who are weary and heavy laden there is the promise of rest; but the general invitation is to heroic enterprise involving readiness for the completest self-sacrifice, and concern for the mere saving of the soul is condemned as a sure way of losing it.

400. LIMITS OF PHILOSOPHY

"Come unto Me . . . and I will give you rest"; it is not Philosophy that can estimate the right of the Speaker to issue that invitation or to make that promise; that right can be proved or disproved only by the experiment of life.

May Thirteenth

401. CITIZENS OF MANKIND

If you have no loyalty in the parish towards the diocese there will not be a great sense of loyalty towards the wider fellowship. People talk easily about being citizens of mankind when they want to escape the obligations of patriotism. In practice it is only through loyalty to the next higher unit than our own that we can effectively serve the wider circle with which we have fellowship.

402. PROPER IMPERIAL PRIDE

Few things are so important for the shaping of imperial policy in the long run as the grounds of the delight which citizens take in the history of country and empire.

403. NATIONAL INTERPRETATIONS OF CHRIST

For we shall never know what Christ is in the fullness of His power until He has all nations at His disposal to manifest through their peculiar gifts the various elements in His all-embracing purpose.

May Fourteenth

404. GOD'S SPECIAL ACTIVITY

It is surely quite clear that if anyone studied the world before there was life on it he could never have predicted life; if he had studied vegetation he would never have predicted animal life; if he had studied the animal world he would never have predicted human civilisation and the arts; and if he had studied the selfishness of mankind he could never have predicted a life of perfect and selfless love. At each stage we reasonably trace the special activity of the Will whose purpose is the explanation of all things.

405. CREDIBILITY OF GOD'S EXISTENCE

The existence of God is fully credible only if evil is being transmuted into good; and that cannot—demonstrably cannot—finally be accomplished unless God the Supreme Good becomes the apparent good to every man. . . . The Supreme Good can only be my apparent good and so dominate my Self if it both is, and, in a form quickening my sympathy, manifestly displays itself as, utterly selfless love.

406. The Holy Spirit in Moral Reaction

This power of God within the soul, responding to God self-manifested in Jesus Christ, could afterwards be recognised in the responsive reaction of all life to the good wherever manifest.

May Fifteenth

407. Practising what You Preach

People often say to a preacher: "Practise what you preach." That is a very wholesome prod for the preacher's conscience; but if the preacher in fact preaches nothing more than he can practise, he is preaching very badly.

408. Extensive and Intensive Church Work

In converting the world, the Church is completing or perfecting itself, extensively, and in conforming the converted world, which is itself, to the standards of the Gospel it is completing or perfecting itself intensively.

409. Preaching and Visiting

The best preaching is a fruit of constant pastoral visiting; it springs out of the relationship between pastor and people.

May Sixteenth

410. Ecclesiastical "Parties"

It is to my mind entirely desirable that there should be in the Church what are sometimes called "schools of thought" and sometimes "parties." What is altogether undesirable is that through the existence of parties there should arise the spirit of partisanship, in which the members of the different groups in the one fellowship tend to regard each other as opponents instead of colleagues—not comrade-regiments in one army, as they truly are, but in some way opposing armies.

411. Heresy and Hypocrisy

For the Church, commissioned to transmit to all generations the true doctrine which may elicit saving faith, heresy is more deadly than hypocrisy or even than conscious sin; but for the individual the one vital matter is personal trust, and accepted heresy in its effect upon his soul may be quite unimportant. There have been saintly heretics and orthodox worldlings.

412. FREEDOM OF THE CHURCH
It is all very well to say that the Church must maintain its freedom in things spiritual at all costs. But actual freedom to carry on spiritual work may depend upon the means of doing it; and the assertion of a principle may involve the loss of opportunity to act on that principle.

May Seventeenth

413. EUCHARISTIC OBLATIONS
In the Holy Communion service we take the bread and wine—man's industrial and commercial life in symbol—and offer it to God; because we have offered it to Him, He gives it back to us as the means of nurturing us. . . . And as we receive it back from Him, we share it with one another in true fellowship. If we think of the service in this way, it is a perfect picture of what secular society ought to be.

414. EUCHARISTIC SACRIFICE: MY BLOOD
"The blood of the covenant" was beyond all possibility of question a sacrificial phrase. The blood was the life offered in sacrifice. He was offering His life in sacrifice—consecrated to God and received by His brethren.

415. FASTING COMMUNION
To say, as some have done, that to receive the Holy Communion after breaking fast is a mortal sin is either to use language loosely (which in such a context is shocking levity) or else must, as I think, be pronounced to be in the proper, though of course not in the vulgar, sense idolatrous, for it involves a conception of God incompatible with the revelation in Jesus Christ.

May Eighteenth

416. FORMATION OF CHARACTER
It was not some Socialist fanatic, but that prince of orthodox economists of the later nineteenth century, Marshall, who said that the two strongest influences in forming the moral character

of citizens are the religious beliefs in which they are trained and the economic system in which they grow up.

417. FALSE FREEDOM

So long as men base their attachment to freedom on the opportunity which it brings to follow their own choice or purpose, so long will freedom and democracy deserve at least some measure of denunciation.

418. STATE AND RELIGION

The spiritual function of the State is not to regulate religion but to make free scope for it and to uphold the regulations made for its expression by the religious associations themselves.

May Nineteenth

419. PREDESTINATION AND INITIATIVE

The man to whom divine control is not the major premise of a dialectical process but a dominating fact of intimate experience does not settle down inertly to watch the activity of that control; the consciousness of control is itself an overmastering impulse, urging him to incredible enterprises and impossible endeavours.

420. ELECTION

We cannot escape the doctrine of Election in some form; it is not so much an inference as the only possible reading of the facts when Theism is accepted.

421. CONVERSION

The worst things that happen do not happen because a few people are monstrously wicked, but because most people are like us. When we grasp that, we begin to realise that our need is not merely for moving quietly on in the way we are going; our need is for radical change, to find a power that is going to turn us into somebody else. That is what the Gospel offers to do.

May Twentieth

422. INSULT

You cannot insult a man more atrociously than by offering him a lower standard than your own.

423. PERSUASION

You can never persuade anybody of anything unless you first recognise the truth in the position which he holds and admit it, or, indeed, if possible, strongly assert it.

424. A PRINCIPLE OF ARGUMENT

It is never right to rest content with disproving another man's view. You must always go on to ask why he held it. You must say, "He is sure to have got hold of something important; he put it wrong, but what was it he had got hold of?"

May Twenty-first

425. THEISTIC REINFORCEMENT IN MORALS

It is one of the chief practical advantages of a theistic belief in the moral sphere, that it enables people not specially sensitive in ethical matters by natural endowment, to feel towards the claims of duty as the most sensitive feel towards them without that added stimulus.

426. EATING FOR PLEASURE

To eat for pleasure, when there is no need for nourishment, is wrong, unless the quantity thus eaten is so small as to be negligible for purposes of nourishment. Wholesome desire is never only for pleasure, but for some object or the satisfaction of some need.

427. WILL AND WISHES

If the will is set on selfish ambitions or carnal pleasures, the fact that it is set precludes it from changing its direction; it cannot change, because it does not will to change; if it did will to change, that would itself be the change. Of course there may be a most sincere wish to change; but that is different; it is something that may become a constituent part of a will to good; but so long as there are also present any forms of wish to enjoy what is evil, with motive power at all approximating to the wish for good, there are only two incompatible wishes, and no real or effective will.

May Twenty-second

428. CONSERVATISM OF THE PROPHETS

Every prophet's appeal is not to a new principle, but to a new application of an old principle, so that he often presents himself as urging a return to the better ways of past generations. Few radical reformers can hope for great success who are unable to present themselves with perfect honesty as the only true conservatives.

429. CHARACTERISTICS OF CHRISTIAN DIVISIONS

Northern Protestantism needs the Roman instinct for order to save it from the chaotic licence of fissiparous sectarianism; Rome needs the Northern love of liberty to save it from the petrifaction of a bureaucratic despotism; the practical and efficient West needs the mysticism and philosophy of the East to save it from materialism; while the subtle and penetrating philosophy of the East seems to need the ethical energy of the West to save it from stagnation or brooding inactivity.

430. DUTY OF REFORMERS

It does not seem to me possible to doubt that the Reformers were bound by loyalty to Christ to preach the truth in Him as they had newly come to know it, and if that could not be inside the unity of the Church, then it must be outside.

May Twenty-third

431. CHRISTIAN PROGRESS

It is certainly a mistake to begin with the picture of a supposedly ideal system and try to establish it. The way of Christian progress is to ask where an existing system is breaking down and readjust it in the light of Christian principles.

432. EXPLOITING THE EARTH

The treatment of the earth by man the exploiter is not only imprudent but sacrilegious. We are not likely to correct our hideous mistakes in this realm unless we can recover the mystical sense of our one-ness with nature. I labour this precisely because many people think it fantastic; I think it is fundamental to sanity.

433. Vested Interests of Labour and Capitalists

It is as difficult to overcome the vested interests of Labour organisations, and those who gain a living by working them, as it is to overcome the capitalist vested interests which Labour rightly denounces. The source of the trouble is not wealth; it is sin—which is the perquisite of no class, and (incidentally) besets us who are ecclesiastical officials as much as others.

May Twenty-fourth

434. Art: a Definition

The conferring of spiritual quality upon inorganic matter, of which the bare possibility is sometimes denied, is one of the commonest experiences of life; the phrase is almost a definition of Art.

435. Arts and Science

Until the last war our system of education was disproportionately literary; there was urgent need to redress the balance by giving a new prominence to scientific studies. As usually happens in human affairs, the reaction has gone too far.

436. Forgetfulness of Self

"To thine own self be true" is a piece of high-class ethical futility which Shakespeare appropriately puts into the mouth of his own most priceless old dotard. The first condition of attainment in Science or Art or Religion is not loyalty to self, but forgetfulness of self in concentration on the Object; it is more truly the meek who possess the earth.

May Twenty-fifth

437. Frustration

The one complete cure for the sense of frustration and futility is to know and to do the will of God. Everyone to whom this becomes a reality is at once supplied with a purpose in life and one which covers the whole of life.

438. Problem of Evil

We totally misconceive alike the philosophic and the practical problem of evil if we picture it as the winning of control over lawless and therefore evil passions by a righteous but insufficiently powerful reason or spirit. It is the spirit which is evil; it is reason which is perverted; it is aspiration itself which is corrupt.

439. Force of Example
The young soul, still plastic and rather timidly making its adventure in the world, sees that others fend for themselves, and resolves to do the like; it also finds that in a world so conducted it is likely to be overwhelmed unless it does the like. However small its own perversion, resulting from its own finitude, may have been, it is firmly rooted in self as its centre by its intercourse with others who were perhaps at the outset in their own outlook and estimate of the goods of life no more perverted than itself.

May Twenty-sixth

440. Limitations of Religion
There is a great danger as well as a deep truth in the contemporary realisation that all religions have a common cause against secularism. For while it is certainly true that all religions posit a spiritual interpretation of the universe . . . it is by no means true that any religion is better than none. A strong case could be made for the contention that on the whole Religion, up to date, had done more harm than good.

441. Mediator
To rely on a supposedly direct communion with God in detachment from all external aids is to expose the soul to suggestions arising from its distortion as well as to those arising from the God whom it would apprehend. Mediation there must be; imagery there must be. If we do not deliberately avail ourselves of the true Mediator we shall be at the mercy of some unworthy medium.

442. False Teaching
It has not been uncommon to find children who, as a result of their religious instruction, feel quite differently towards God and Christ. When that occurs, it proves that their teaching has been grievously at fault.

May Twenty-seventh

443. JUSTIFICATION OF SELF-CENTREDNESS

When love by its own sacrifice has converted self-centredness into love, there is an excellence, alike in the process and in the result, so great as to justify the self-centredness and all the welter of evil flowing from it.

444. JUDGMENT AND REDEMPTION

His purpose is not judgment but redemption. But judgment follows the offer of redemption. He who has heard and rejected the Gospel is not in the same position as one who has never heard it. The message which he heard is his accuser.

445. REPENTANCE AND JOY

To repent is to adopt God's viewpoint in place of your own. There need not be any sorrow about it. In itself, far from being sorrowful, it is the most joyful thing in the world, because when you have done it you have adopted the viewpoint of truth itself, and you are in fellowship with God. It means a complete re-valuation of all things we are inclined to think good. The world, as we live in it, is like a shop window in which some mischievous person has got overnight and shifted all the price-labels round so that the cheap things have the high price-labels on them, and the really precious things are priced low. We let ourselves be taken in. Repentance means getting those price-labels back in the right place.

May Twenty-eighth

446. BELIEF IN GOD

If when a man says, "I believe in God," what he really means is, "I suppose there is some sort of God somewhere," it is quite unimportant whether he holds that opinion or its opposite. But the opening words of the Creed do not mean that; they mean, "I put my trust in God."

447. RELIGION AND THE INTELLECT

Intellectual acceptance even of correct doctrine is not by itself vital religion; orthodoxy is not identical with the fear or the love of God. This fact of the inadequacy of the truest doctrine is a warning that to argue syllogistically from doctrinal formulæ is to court disaster. The formula may be the best possible; yet it is only a label used to designate a living thing.

448. MIND AND EVENT
The essence of revelation is intercourse of mind and event, not the communication of doctrine distilled from that intercourse.

May Twenty-ninth

449. CHRISTIAN TEACHING
There is a temptation, now that Theism in a general sense is again entirely respectable, to content ourselves with teaching which evokes a comfortable spiritual warmth, but stops short of that which alone can kindle fire.

450. FAULTY TRAINING FOR MINISTRY
Our training for the ministry has been too exclusively pastoral in its outlook and insufficiently evangelistic; that is to say, it has aimed at enabling men to foster the spiritual life of those who are within the Church, but has not sufficiently equipped them to make appeal with power to those who are outside.

451. THE WORK OF THE CLERGY
It is quite impossible to leave the responsibility of Christian witness in respect of most practical problems to the clergy. They have not the requisite knowledge; but beside this, they have an outlook which is specialised in an irrelevant direction. None the less they have a real function in this connection; it is, not to formulate policies, but to stimulate in the laity a sense of responsibility and remind them of the claims of their Christian faith in the various departments of life. But the actual leavening of the world's lump with the energies of the Kingdom of Heaven must be done by laymen.

May Thirtieth

452. SPHERE OF ABSOLUTE OBLIGATION

Universal obligation attaches not to particular judgments of conscience but to conscientiousness. What acts are right may depend on circumstances, social history and context, personal relationships, and a host of other considerations. But there is an absolute obligation to will whatever may on each occasion be right.

453. LOVE AND PARTICULAR ACTS

Particular acts derive their value from their capacity to promote or to hinder the best relations between people, the relationship which must express their personality. All particular commands or prohibitions derive their value from their tendency to promote or to hinder the relationship of love on the widest possible scale.

454. DESIRE OF EVIL

To desire evil strictly for its own sake is impossible. To hate the human race so as to desire as good for one's self what is evil for all others, and even because it is evil for all others, is possible; but this evil for others is still desired as supposedly good for him who desires it.

May Thirty-first

455. PROGRESS

The whole process of social and civic development is the parallel growth of two things: the richness of individual personality with completeness of social intercourse. The development of personality in fellowship is no bad definition of what we mean by progress.

456. INTERNATIONAL JUSTICE

It is commonly laid down as a principle of justice that no man should be judge in his own cause; and I believe that one of the chief necessities, if justice is to be established and with it a hope of peace, is that all nations should forgo the right to judge their own cause.

457. NATIONALISATION

There may be some industries which are best conducted by management directly responsible to the State, as the Post Office is. But this should probably be rare and confined to services indispensable to the whole community. For State management involves bureaucracy, and this easily becomes as stifling to free personality as grinding competition.

JUNE

June First

458. CREED AND CHARACTER

What we cannot expect to happen is that our characters are going to change through our holding an opinion which we keep somewhere in a pigeon-hole of the mind merely to be brought out on demand. You say the Creed; the words, "I believe in God," do not mean, "I incline to the opinion that in all probability there exists a Being who may not inappropriately be called God." You mean, "I put my trust in that union of power and goodness." You mean, "I undertake to live as if these things were so." If you do not mean that, you ought not to say the Creed.

459. MENTAL IDOLATRY

Any image of God is inadequate; but what people often fail to observe is that when, instead of making the image out of material things, you make it out of thoughts, if you make it yourself, it will be equally inadequate, and it is just as much idolatry to worship God according to a false mental image as by means of a false metal image.

460. VEHICLE OF KNOWLEDGE OF GOD

Knowledge of God can be fully given to man only in a person, never in a doctrine, still less in a formless faith, whatever that might be.

June Second

461. THE LEVEL OF FAITH

Faith is the property of the Church, not of the individual alone. And as, on the one side, we pray, "Regard not our sins but the faith of Thy Church," so on the other side we must confess our inability to rise far above the level of faith in the Church of our day. We must do what we can to raise that level of faith, but we must not pretend that we are independent of it.

462. THREE ENEMIES

Hatred of the world is hard to face. The world is the most dangerous of the three great enemies. In our conflict with the flesh and the devil the world itself in a civilised country gives us some support. But against the world we must stand alone with our fellow Christians.

463. WORLD'S HATRED

The world would not hate angels for being angelic; but it does hate men for being Christians. It grudges them their new character; it is tormented by their peace; it is infuriated by their joy.

June Third

464. FORGIVENESS: HOW OFTEN?

We are apt to say, "I have befriended so and so three times over, and I do not think anyone can expect me to do any more." And we like our friends to say, "No, my dear, I do not think they can." St. Peter knows three times will not be enough. Will seven times do? No; four hundred and ninety; more times than it is conceivable that one man should injure another. Why? It means that there is no rule about it; but if there is the spirit of God in your heart you will want to forgive him every time; the question will not arise.

465. JOY OF FORGIVEN SINNER

The forgiven sinner who rejoices chiefly in his own forgiven state has not fully appropriated the forgiveness offered or fully escaped from the sin which called for it. The fully forgiven man does not rejoice in his own forgiveness but in the divine love to which he owes it; and his past sin persists in his experience no longer as a source of shame but as the occasion of a new wonder in his adoration of the love divine.

466. SCORN

Next time you feel inclined to despise somebody and say he is really not worth the smallest attention, remember that Christ thought it worth while to die for him.

467. GOD'S BLESSINGS

If all our wants are supplied while we have no thought of God this may confirm us in our detachment from Him, and so the things that should have been for our wealth are unto us an occasion of falling. Consequently the question whether what is normally a blessing, such as deliverance from the enticement of some temptation, will be in actual fact a blessing to me may often depend on whether or not I recognise God as the source of all good things. So the first requirement in prayer is that we trust to God for all blessing.

468. THE GLORY OF GOD

When we come into our Father's presence, our Lord seems to say, we should be so filled with the thought of Him that we forget all about ourselves, our hopes, our needs, even our sins; what we want most of all and therefore utter first is that all men may know how glorious God is and reverence Him accordingly—"Hallowed be Thy Name."

469. GOD'S WILL

Our first thought must never be, "What can I do for God?" The answer to that is, "Nothing." The first thought must always be, "What would God do for me?"

June Fifth

470. FATAL DEVOTION

If your conception of God is radically false, then the more devout you are the worse it will be for you. You are opening your soul to be moulded by something base. You had much better be an atheist.

471. SELFISH SPENDING

What men spend on acts of worship is spent on what they share, and the gift may therefore be infected with self-interest. We ought to offer to God in worship the best music that we can. But our subscription to the organ fund at our Church is likely to be more self-regarding than our support of a mission in a place we shall never see; for we ourselves shall enjoy the music.

472. GOING TO CHURCH

If you go to Church, for example, only to stand there while somebody else sings hymns, and kneel there—or more probably, not kneel, but adopt that astonishingly uncomfortable and completely undevotional attitude which is so familiar—while someone says prayers, how can you expect it to have any effect on you except a deadening one? But if we open our hearts to the reality that is there, and, if there seems to be not much reality, at least bring some of your own, then we shall begin to live up to our profession, which is to follow our Saviour Christ and be made like unto Him.

June Sixth

473. GOD'S INITIATIVE

Our love is cold. It is there, but it is feeble. It does not carry us to real obedience. Is there anything that I can do? No; there never is, except to hold myself in His presence; the initiative remains with God. But the Lord, who knows both the reality and the poverty of our love, will supply our need.

474. PRAYER AND CONDUCT

The range of a Christian's fruitful activity is far greater through his prayer, that is the direction of his will, surrendered as it is to God, than through his conduct or direct influence.

475. HIS NAME

To ask in His name is to ask as His representative, or in other words, according to His will. We acknowledge Him as the source of the blessing, so that its bestowal will bind us more closely to Him, not make us forgetful of Him; and as what is asked is what He already desires to give, the gift follows upon the fulfilment of this condition.

June Seventh

476. PRIORITIES IN PRAYER

Do you care at all whether God is honoured and reverenced "in earth as in heaven"? You cannot offer a truly Christian prayer for daily bread or for forgiveness unless you have prayed for God's honour and glory; for Christ Himself put this first of all petitions.

477. THANKING GOD

It is more important to thank God for blessings received than to pray for them beforehand. For that forward-looking prayer, though right as an expression of dependence upon God, is still self-centred in part, at least, of its interest; there is something which we hope to gain by our prayer. But the backward-looking act of thanksgiving is quite free from this. In itself it is quite selfless. Thus it is akin to love.

478. PERSEVERANCE IN PRAYER

There is nothing that so much develops faith as to persevere in asking through disappointment. If you always get the blessing you seek at once, or something you recognise as corresponding to it, your faith will remain at about the level at which you started. The reason why God calls for perseverance is not, of course, that He wishes to test our faith. He knows exactly what it is worth. But He may wish to deepen it. The thing that will most deepen it is to persist with faith through disappointment.

June Eighth

479. WITNESS

A real Christian, who abides in Christ and Christ in him, exerts an influence among his companions at work or play, in mine or shop or factory or directors' meeting or Parliament, that nothing effaces.

480. TRUSTING GOD

Is my love feeble? Let me deepen communion by deliberate obedience. But what kind of obedience is it? Are we to "do" this, and avoid "doing" that? No; that is the way of the law and

117

its works. Our obedience is to the commandments of the Lord, which are—to trust God and to love Him.

481. GOD'S GLORY

Our success, or health, or welfare is of very small importance in itself; only because God loves us, unlovely as we are, have we value in ourselves; that value is our value to Him; and what gives importance to our well-being is that it brings glory to God.

June Ninth

482. HUMANISM

Humanism consists, roughly speaking, in the acceptance of many Christian standards of life with a rejection or neglect of the only sources of power to attain to them.

483. APPREHENSION OF REALITY

What the mind apprehends, even when it apprehends mistakenly, is reality; the true apprehension of reality is attained not at the beginning but at the end of the mental process.

484. REALITY DISCOVERED

In the progressive conquest of the unknown by the mind of man there is at every stage the satisfaction of success; but the great and lasting joy is not in the discovery of reality, it is in the reality discovered.

June Tenth

485. LIGHT IN THE CHURCH

The Christian joy and hope do not arise from an ignoring of the evil in the world, but from facing it at its worst. The light that shines for ever in the Church breaks out of the veriest pit of gloom.

486. THE MEDIATOR

The Son is the Mediator, through whom our prayers ascend to the Father and through whom the Father's love descends in blessings on His children. This does not interpose a barrier between God and Man, for the Mediator is Himself both God and

Man. Another way of approaching this thought would be to say that through the union of divine and human in Jesus Christ, we have both more assured access to the Father and more abundant blessing from the Father.

487. Spirit and Regulations
Religious ordinances are to be used according to the benefit to be derived from them, according to the movement of the free spirit, and not according to the rigid enforcement of regulations.

June Eleventh

488. Limitations of Science
Scientific inquiry now gives us a universe which was once very, very hot, and is going to be some day very cold; how it got there or how it became hot it cannot explain.

489. Corollary of Science
It would seem strangely paradoxical to say that though science is a product of the mind as appreciative of value, yet value and appreciation have no ultimate significance or importance in that real world which science apprehends.

490. Scientist and Theologian
The theologian who quarrels with science on its own ground is but a presumptuous fool. But the scientist who quarrels with theology on its own ground is no better. If there is mutual respect and common reverence for truth in all its forms there may still be divergence and even what we have called tension; but there will be no quarrel.

June Twelfth

491. Holy Spirit
Truth, when we speak of knowing it, is the objective reality as it actually is, undistorted and completely apprehended; truth as a quality of the mind is sincerity, which includes positively the desire to apprehend reality completely and accurately, and negatively the absence of conflicting interests which may bias or blur the judgment. The Comforter is the source of both kinds of truth.

492. Coming of the Kingdom

The Kingdom cannot come in all its perfection in this world for at least two reasons. First, it is a fellowship of all generations; secondly, every child that is born, being a nucleus of that Original Sin which is self-centredness, disturbs such degree of approximation as has been reached.

493. Theology and Science

It is our duty and the supreme need to make the word "theology" and what it stands for as familiar and as little frightening as the word "science"; so that of the one as of the other everyone should feel that he must know enough for practical purposes of life and should know where to go if he needs more, and that of the one as of the other what he does know is sound and well-informed.

June Thirteenth

494. False Economics

The result of trusting to the profit-motive has been the strange phenomenon of "poverty in the midst of plenty"; and the only solution proposed by those who rely on the profit-motive is to abolish the plenty! During the nineteenth century the essentially false basis of our economic structure was concealed by the apparently limitless expansion of markets. Search for profits led to increased production; and this always found a market somewhere.

495. Profit Motive

In one way or another it should be secured that no one, by investing capital alone, can become possessed of a permanent and saleable right to levy a tax upon the enterprise in which he invests his money together with a voice in the control of it. Thus the grip of profit-seeking capital upon industry will be loosened.

496. Bank of England

We all have reason to be grateful for the stability of our banking system and for the ability and integrity with which it is administered. Yet it cannot be justified in modern conditions that the banks, even the Bank of England, should, in order to meet national needs, create credit which earns interest for themselves. . . .

A body within the community controls what is vital to the welfare of the community; and that is a false principle.

June Fourteenth

497. OVERFLOWING LOVE

It makes a vast difference whether we suppose that God loves us because we are lovable, or that He loves us, in spite of much in us which deserves His antagonism, because He is overflowing love.

498. CHRISTIAN OBEDIENCE

We are to love our neighbours as ourselves, and our fellow Christians as Christ loved us. These commands cannot be obeyed with the same precision as commands to go to Church or to give a tenth of income for Church work. The commands of Christ will nearly always carry these and similar actions as incidental consequences of the obedience claimed, but they go beyond anything of this kind.

499. HEAVEN

These *many resting-places*, marking the stages of our spiritual growth, are in the *Father's house*. If we are travelling heavenwards, we are already in heaven.

June Fifteenth

500. IMPERSONAL ANGER

Our moral antagonism to the spirit of those who oppose us is so much mixed up with the emotional reaction of our offended self-concern that we are almost incapable of impersonal anger— the dreadful anger of perfect love at hate or selfishness.

501. USING RELIGION

We are all under the temptation to call in Christian faith as a means of delivering us from the agony of war, caring more for our own escape from that torture than for God's glory. It is very natural; it is a state of mind with which we must all sympathise; but it is at best sub-Christian.

502. MISSIONARY CHRISTIANS

His gift of Himself, that is to say of perfect love, is not something which you can have and keep. If you are keeping it, it proves you have not got it. Every Christian is a missionary, and if he is not a missionary he is not yet truly or deeply a Christian at all.

June Sixteenth

503. SPIRITUAL SUBMISSION

If a man accepts some doctrine of the Church, though he himself has no perception of the truth of that doctrine and conforms solely on the ground that he thinks the Church likely to be right, that submission to its authority is fully spiritual; it is a free exercise of judgment concerning the good.

504. RESPONSIBILITY OF DISUNION

The guilt of the sin of disunion rests upon us all, not less on those who have maintained the historic order and failed to commend it than on those who for conscience' sake broke away from it.

505. PENAL REFORM

If I were asked to point to any great achievement of the Church in England in the twentieth century so far as it has gone, I should point without hesitation to the reform of our penal administration.

June Seventeenth

506. SACRIFICE IN AND WITH CHRIST

In every Eucharist . . . we repeat His actions that we may enter into their meaning, receiving the Life He offered in sacrifice that in its power we may offer ourselves a sacrifice in union with His. That, for me, is the heart of the matter.

507. LOCAL SYMBOLS OF EUCHARIST

The Bread and the Wine are the local symbols by which is made specially accessible to us Christ in His sacrifice, who by reason of that sacrifice is seated at the right hand of God, and is therefore everywhere as God is everywhere.

508. Devotions before the Blessed Sacrament

If, when the consecrated Elements are reserved, devout persons find help in praying where they have before them these symbols and vehicles of Christ's self-giving, I see no reason why they should not do so. . . . But there are real dangers; and the dangers are so grave and so near at hand that I think the Church does well to forbid the holding of any service in connection with the Elements reserved.

June Eighteenth

509. Being in Christ

All that we can ask in His name is that we may really do His will and bear fruit for the Lord of the vineyard. We ask whatsoever we will; but being in Christ our will must be for the glory of God and the accomplishment of His purpose.

510. His Will

So often we get far enough to prefer His will to ours in principle; but we are not in communion with Him close enough to avoid insisting upon our judgment of what His will must be—like Peter and Cæsarea Phillipi or at the feet-washing.

511. First Duty

Every disciple and every company of disciples begin by wanting to give service. No doubt it is wise that the Church should, as far as possible, provide opportunities for this. But every disciple and every company of disciples need to learn that their first duty is to let Christ serve them.

June Nineteenth

512. Moral Obligation

Summary of moral obligation: Your being is personal; live as a person in fellow-membership with all others who, being personal, are your fellow members in the community of persons. Strive to grow in fullness of personality, in width and depth of fellowship; and seek to draw the energy for this from that to which you and all things owe their origin, the Personal Love which is Creator and Sustainer of the world.

513. Honesty and Penalties

Even those of us who are usually honest on principle and by preference, are occasionally saved from lapses into dishonesty by the penalties attached to it when detected.

514. Exceptional Circumstances and Rules

Nothing so much imperils a general rule as to enlist in opposition to it the generosity of human nature by a rigid enforcement that takes no account of special circumstances.

June Twentieth

515. My Work

Apart from Him, I can do nothing. All fruit that I ever bear or can bear comes wholly from His life within me. No particle of it is mine as distinct from His. There is, no doubt, some part of His whole purpose that He would accomplish through me; that is my work, my fruit, in the sense that I, and not another, am the channel of His life for this end; but in no other sense.

516. Present Judgment

It is not said that if we do not abide in Christ we shall subsequently or ultimately be cast out of the vineyard on to the fire; what is said is that our failure to abide in Him is, there and then, that rejection and destruction.

517. Removing Mountains

I believe that faith makes available for man all the infinite resources of Almighty God, so that by faith a man could literally walk on the water or remove mountains.

June Twenty-first

518. Seat of Sin

The seat of sin is the very organ of our moral improvement and of our communion with God. It is in the spiritual life itself, and that is why we cannot cure it. It is a corruption in the very capacity of aspiration. In some degree the light which is in us is darkness.

519. THE PERVERSION OF REASON

Man's "sin" is not a mere survival or disproportionate development of animal tendencies, or an inadequate development of rational control. It is a perversion of reason itself. His capacity for divine communion is become a usurpation of divine authority. The worst, most typical sin, from which all other sin flows, is not sensuality but pride.

520. SPIRITUAL FALSE PERSPECTIVES

Because mind is finite it attaches undue importance to those goods and evils which it apprehends as affecting itself; its perspectives are falsified; what is near at hand looks larger than it is, and what is far off, smaller than it is.

June Twenty-second

521. PROCREATION

The sexual function of men and women is primarily that whereby they co-operate with God in the creation of His children; that is why they are said to procreate—to act on behalf of the Creator.

522. V.D.

Almost exclusively, this disease is contracted as a result of what is now called "promiscuous intercourse," but in the Bible and the Prayer Book is called "fornication." I think we have done harm by being so polite about these things. It is better to use the old language which disgusts people just because it disgusts them; for the thing is disgusting. All sexual indulgence outside matrimony is contrary to God's law and is sin. Let us be ready to say so.

523. PROPHYLACTICS

If I am rightly informed, one of the best records for immunity from venereal disease held by any unit of our Forces in the 1914-1918 War was that of a Canadian regiment in which no prophylactics were issued nor instruction in the use of them given, but ablution centres were provided; any man who thought he might have become infected was expected to make use of these, and actually to contract the disease was treated as a serious military offence.

524. COMMUNION OF SAINTS

Eternal life is the life of love—not primarily of being loved, but of loving, admiring, and (in love and admiration) forgetting self. Such a life is not only an entering into, but is the actual building of, that fellowship of mutually enriching selves which we have called the Commonwealth of Value.

525. LIFE AND RESURRECTION

Fellowship with Christ is participation in the divine life which finds its fullest expression in triumph over death. Life is a larger word than Resurrection; but Resurrection is, so to speak, the crucial quality of Life.

526. JOY OF ATTAINMENT

The mind or soul that is set on an object capable of truly feeding it may still, and perhaps for ever, suffer the pain of expansion, as it seeks to absorb a proffered wealth to which its capacity is unequal, but that pain is accompanied and transmuted by the joy of perpetual attainment.

June Twenty-fourth

527. THE CLOSED HEART

We may go to Church and say our prayers and read our Bibles; the cleansing Word flows over us; but if our hearts are closed we are not cleansed. And the Lord knows the man that is betraying Him, perhaps before that man knows it himself. So of every company of Christians He may be saying, *Ye are not all clean.* Let each of us ask tremblingly, Lord is it I?

528. DISCIPLINE AND LAW

Our discipline is not a bracing of our wills to conformity with a law; it is the maintenance of communion with the Lord to the point of mutual indwelling . . . But though our discipline is not conformity with a code, it is obedience to a commandment; for "this is His commandment, that we should believe the name of His Son Jesus Christ and love one another."

529. ABIDING IN CHRIST

Abide in Me and I in you. All truth and depth of devotion, all effectiveness in service spring from this. It is not a theme for words, but for the deeper apprehensions of silence.

June Twenty-fifth

530. SACREDNESS OF PERSONALITY AND COMMUNITY

The sacredness of personality might work out as a kind of egoism all round if it were not at once balanced by the other great principle of fellow membership, that we belong to one another.

531. UNDEVELOPED WILL

The schoolboy is often a different person in his home and at school, in the headmaster's drawing-room and among rowdy companions. For this he is sometimes accused of hypocrisy; but that is unjust; both groups of reaction are perfectly spontaneous and sincere; and to treat such a boy as if he deliberately adapted himself to his surroundings would be profoundly mistaken. He is not to be treated as having a perverted will, but as having a will incompletely formed.

532. SELF-PROPOSED IDEAL

Sometimes by a natural process of compensation those who are most selfless in the search for truth or beauty, or in public service, are most selfish, fretful and querulous at home. No ideal which a man purposes to himself will deliver him from the tyranny of self.

June Twenty-sixth

533. POLITICS AND GAMES

The whole arena of politics belongs to a class of activities which is less important than the class to which games belong. I do not say that politics are less important than games, because they are means to more important ends, while games are a less important end. And so politics are of more importance; but they belong to that particular class which exist for something beyond themselves. That is supremely true of the economic part of political life; it is all concerned with the means by which men are to pursue virtue, religion and happiness.

534. ECONOMIC LIMITATIONS
There are real ends in life, and they are all in that realm which belongs to us in virtue of our spiritual and intellectual capacities, and not of our animal capacities. They all belong to the realm, for example, either of knowledge, or appreciation of beauty, or friendship, or family affection or loyalties, and courage, and love and joy and peace. . . . The whole economic sphere is concerned with means to those ends; and it must be judged, not primarily by its efficiency within itself; . . . but primarily in the light of the question whether it is fostering the attainment of the real ends by the greatest number of people. We may take as our slogan, if you like: "Fullness of Personality in the widest possible Fellowship."

535. THE AVERAGE CITIZEN
I believe the profoundest discussion of political philosophy extant is that in which Plato maintains that a political constitution or a social organisation is inevitably the reproduction on a large scale of the value-judgments of the average citizen.

June Twenty-seventh

536. LIMITATIONS OF INFALLIBILITY
Infallible direction for practical action is not to be had either from Bible or Church or Pope or individual communing with God; and this is not through any failure of a wise and loving God to supply it, but because in whatever degree reliance upon such infallible direction comes in, spirituality goes out. Intelligent and responsible judgment is the privilege and burden of spirit or personality.

537. CHRISTIAN RESPONSIBILITY
Christians must exercise their own insight and their own intelligence, not only in judging whether or not to submit themselves to Him as Lord, but also in estimating the claim on their allegiance of any particular recorded direction.

538. ANGLICANISM AND PERSONAL FREEDOM
The characteristic of our Church is to offer to men in all its wealth and fullness the inheritance of the Catholic Church,

inviting them to come and take their full share in it, but leaving them always in the last resort to decide.

June Twenty-eighth

539. JUDGMENT AND WAR

The City of God, which has sometimes appeared as a beleaguered fortress, again stands before us with gates wide open so that citizens of all nations may enter, but also that its own citizens may ride forth to the conquest of the nations, following their Captain as He goes forth to judge and to make war.

540. UNITY WITHIN THE CHURCH

We have to make strong the bonds of our own unity, with gratitude for our splendid inheritance, so that we may bring to the universal Church a life strong in faith, in order, in corporate devotion— maintaining all that we have received but recognising also God's gifts to His people through traditions other than our own.

541. THE SPIRIT IN THE CHURCH

It is no true loyalty to the mind of the Lord which confines attention to what He did and said on earth. Then He kept His teaching within the range of His disciples' apprehension. . . . We are most loyal to the mind of Christ when we are most receptive of all that the Apostles, under the guidance of the Spirit, learnt and taught, and of all that the same Spirit would teach us now.

June Twenty-ninth

542. "CHANGING GOD'S MIND"

We are not, in our prayers, trying to suggest to God something He has not thought of. That would plainly be ridiculous. Nor are we trying to change His mind. That would be an enterprise blasphemous in the attempt, and calamitous in the accomplishment.

543. MEDIATION

Nothing is more precious in the spiritual life than that communion with God which is enjoyed when the soul reposes upon God in utter self-abandonment, and God exercises His moulding power upon the soul thus resting, plastic, in His hands. . . . But it never is unmediated. It is mediated by all our thought of God, as this has come to us through our home-life, through natural beauty, through conscience (itself a focus of our moral tradition), through acts of worship, through Jesus the Word of God.

544. AUTO-SUGGESTION AND PRAYER
When the psychologist tells us that our methods of prayer and worship are means of auto-suggestion, we shall say: "Of course they are; and if there exists a God who is our loving Father, what can be wiser or more reasonable than that we should, by methods well tried and proved, bring home to our souls His reality and His love?"

June Thirtieth

545. GRACE OF GOD
When I want to move my hand, it moves. I don't have to stop and think, "How shall I move it?" It happens. But if I find myself to be a selfish kind of person and want to be unselfish, it doesn't happen. Therefore, something has got to take hold of us from outside.

546. LOVING THE SON
The Father loves all His children with an infinite love. Yet there is a special love also in His heart for those who love that Son. The universal love of God is not a featureless uniformity of goodwill. Goodwill to all there is; but also for each whatever special quality of love is appropriate to him; and there must be a special quality of love for those who love the Son.

547. THE VINE
The vine lives to give its life-blood. Its flower is small, its fruit abundant; and when that fruit is mature and the vine has for a moment become glorious, the treasure of the grapes is torn down and the vine is cut back to the stem—

> and next year blooms again,
> Not bitter for the torment undergone,
> Not barren for the fullness yielded up.

JULY

July First

548. INSPIRATION

He guides the process; He guides the minds of men; the interaction of the process and the minds which are alike guided by Him is the essence of revelation.

549. MECHANICAL CONSTANCY AND GOD'S ACTION

His action in guiding the world is not constant in a mechanical sense; rather its constancy, as that of all personal action, is found in its infinite adjustability to present conditions. . . . Among the conditions are the attitudes adopted by, and the situations created by, the relatively free acts of finite intelligences like ourselves.

550. DIVINE TRANSCENDENCE

What a true doctrine of divine transcendence will assert is not a reservoir of normally unutilised energy, but a volitional as contrasted with a mechanical direction of the energy utilised.

July Second

551. RAISING SOCIETY

Our capacity to raise society depends upon our being veritable members of it, working for the highest things which we can work for in it, but not cutting ourselves off from it, not standing aside and giving good advice from the touch-line.

552. SCUM AND CREAM

A great deal has been said in praise of competition, and most of it is rubbish. It is said, for example, that you must not interfere with natural processes; you must let the cream come to the top. But the scum comes to the top quite as much as the cream. It is sometimes said that if you want to get the best out of a man you must appeal to his own interest. That brings us to the crucial point. For if that is true, Christ was wrong.

553. ART OF BUILDING

The Bible opens with a series of stories each of which has the same moral; that moral is that whenever men acquire new knowledge, new pleasure, new power, they first make a selfish and therefore a bad use of it. The series culminates in the discovery of the art of building with its new gift of security against the powers of Nature, with resultant independence of God and usurpation of the place of God.

July Third

554. CHURCHMANSHIP

If then the Christian citizen is to make his Christianity tell upon his politics, his business, his social enterprises, he must be a Churchman—consciously belonging to the worshipping fellowship and sharing its worship—before he is a citizen; he must bring the concerns of his citizenship and his business before God, and go forth to them carrying God's inspiration with him.

555. PUBLIC OPINION

When great multitudes of people adopt an idea it may be more false than true, but it is unlikely to be simply and solely false.

556. WRONG PASTORAL MOTIVES

We may come to our pastoral work, the exercise of influence, through love of power and the satisfaction which we derive from guiding others; or through love of fame and repute; or through partisanship, and the desire to win adherents for our own "school of thought." But none of these entitles us to exercise deliberate influence over another. A man who attempts it, is *a thief and a robber*.

July Fourth

557. RIGHT OF OWNERSHIP

The right which attaches to ownership is a right of administration, but should never be a right to exclusive use. That is a principle deep and constant in the old Christian tradition about property, but we have so largely forgotten that property is in its own nature and of necessity a social institution and a social fact, that we have ignored the rights of society over against the rights of those to whom it entrusts ownership, and we must restore that balance.

558. Monopolies

Now it is surely a primary political principle that, when something which is universally necessary becomes a monopoly, that monopoly should be taken under public control; and in my judgment at least—I don't claim that it is worth much, but I want to offer it you—in my judgment at least, it should be now regarded as improper for any private person or corporation to issue new credit, as it was in the Middle Ages for any private person or corporation to mint actual money, for the two are equivalent.

559. Wealth and Power

Acquisitiveness in human nature, which at present expresses itself through unlimited search for material wealth, may just as easily express itself in a collectivised society through the grasping and manipulating of the levers of power. And on the whole that would be more disastrous for the other citizens than what we have at present.

July Fifth

560. Virtue and Fear

Even if nothing sustained the virtuous conduct except fear, it would still be better than vicious conduct, both because it is beneficial instead of harmful to society and because its own excellence at least has the opportunity of making its appeal to the conscience of the person acting, so that imperceptibly another and better foundation for the virtuous conduct may be fashioned.

561. Conscience Unreliable

Conscience, which we here understand as the spontaneous verdict of a man's moral nature, is not by any means a completely reliable guide to life. It may be the best that we have got at any moment, and we must act by it, but always with readiness to revise its judgments.

562. Actual Obligations

Our actual obligations depend on our membership of society and on the character of the society of which we are members. . .

But that does not affect the nature of obligation itself, or the inherent logic which makes it a principle of progress. . . . The sense of obligation to serve the common good as apprehended at any time is inevitably a sense of obligation also to apprehend it better.

July Sixth

563. FAILURE

When we fail in our discipleship it is always for one of two reasons; either we are not trying to be loyal, or else we are trying in our own strength and find that it is not enough.

564. CHRISTIAN PROGRESS

The Lord calls us to absolute perfection; but He points us here and now to what is for each one the next stage, the next *resting-place*, on the way to it. And as we follow, we find Him there to welcome us. More than that—He comes to lead us there.

565. UPWARD CALL

The new "call upwards" is sometimes an awareness of something positively wrong, a "weight" that must be laid aside (Hebrews xii. 1), and sometimes an apprehension of service to be rendered which calls for completer self-devotion.

July Seventh

566. LAMB AND BEAST

In the last resort there are only two pivots about which human life can revolve, and we are always organising society and ourselves about one or other of them. They are self and God. In the great book with which the Bible closes, these two principles are set before us under the symbolic figures of the "Lamb standing, as it had been slain"—the symbol of love that uses sacrifice as its instrument—and the great wild beast, the symbol of self-will or pride, whose instrument is force.

567. LOVE AND "REAL JUSTICE"

While the Church exists to preach love, and the State to maintain justice, the Christian citizen draws on the inspiration of love to establish a closer approximation to real justice.

568. HOSPITALS

Christianity founds hospitals, and atheists are cured in them, never knowing that they owe their cure to Christ.

July Eighth

569. UNITED WITNESS

The Lambeth Conference of 1930 expressly encouraged Joint-Evangelism. Experience shows that this is far more difficult. If two speakers representing different communions have proclaimed the Gospel and appealed for personal decisions, an awkward situation arises when one of their hearers declares himself convinced and asks what he does next. Which speaker is to direct him? This difficulty can be avoided by the method . . . of a united evangelistic campaign conducted in parallel services, but opened with a united service of prayer and closing with a united service of thanksgiving and dedication.

570. COMPETING SECTS

How can we persuade an incredulous world that we have the secret of that unity which overleaps all barriers of religious or cultural inheritance, of economic status or of sex itself, so that we become "one man in Christ Jesus," if we present to that world the appearance of competing sects? The obligation to attain to a real and organic unity of the Church as the Holy Spirit may guide us is urgent; yet it is to be feared that many Church people are almost unaware of it and indifferent to it.

571. MISSION OF CHURCH

The Church in latter years has re-learned how to worship, but not in anything like the same degree how to understand. The congregation expects to gather for worship, it does not expect also to learn.

July Ninth

572. INTERDEPENDENCE OF MATTER, MIND AND SPIRIT

Without the mechanical basis in matter, there could be no life of the kind that we know. Without living matter—bodily organisms—mind, as we know it, does not arise. Without animal mind (seeking means to an end presented as good) there could be no spirit such as we know (choosing between ends by reference to an ideal standard of good).

573. INTERPRETATION OF FACTS

There is no such thing in all human experience as a naked fact. We interpret as we perceive, from earliest infancy. The very process of receiving impressions is always interpretative; and with the interpretation there is the possibility, of course, of mistake.

574. VALUE ALTERS

In respect of value past events, as apprehended in the present, are not unalterable, but may still be so affected by the results won or wrought out of them as to become even the opposite of what at the time of their occurrence they were, and, when viewed in their isolation, still are.

July Tenth

575. ORGANISED SELFISHNESS

Nothing is so important from the point of view of Christianising society as to recognise that competition is not a thing limited to business. It is a thing that pervades the whole of our life. It is simply organised selfishness.

576. THE GREAT DELUSION

The greatest delusion that can possibly seize upon the human mind is the supposition that whatever happens next is bound to be better. We really might have learnt that by now, but it seems many of us have not.

577. STATUS AND CONTRACT

One of the questions that we have got to ask ourselves in these modern times is how far our grandfathers were quite right when they regarded it as sheer gain that we should have moved from the basis of status to a basis of contract.

July Eleventh

578. THE FALL

The human mind has knowledge of good and evil. The winning of that knowledge is called the Fall of Man, because acts, which before he won it were merely instinctive reactions to environment, become through that knowledge sins against the light.

579. Evolution and the Fall

And let us also recognise that the Fall . . . is a quite plain reality on the basis of evolution, as much as it would be on any other theory, because a deliberately cruel man is certainly worse than an instinctively cruel beast.

580. Implications of Self-sacrifice

How can it be that the inner logic of a man's nature should prompt him to ignore his own interest for that of his friend or his country? Does this not mean that man is by his nature shown to be created for love? And does not this again imply that in the ground of his being, and therefore in the ground of that natural order of which he is the most elaborately developed product within our knowledge, there must be the spring of that love which thus wells up in him?

July Twelfth

581. Duty and Divine Companionship

It is no good saying that we should love God with all our hearts—we do not know enough about Him; and your neighbour as yourself, for he will irritate you just as much to-morrow as he did to-day. You cannot suddenly evolve from within yourself the reserve of love which would enable you to accept that irritation, or something more than irritation, from your neighbour, and by enduring whatever it may be, make his fault the occasion of a better love between you. That is the Christian way, but we cannot follow it except in the power of God that grows in our hearts, if we find the companionship of Him in whom alone it is possible.

582. Dependence

Dedication is an activity of our wills, necessary but not ultimate. The chief need of all is that we let our dependence upon God become so living a fact of actual experience that we may be from henceforth channels of His living energy.

583. Consequences of Incarnation

The Nativity, Death and Resurrection of Christ did not make God other than He was before. They did, indeed, enable Him to treat mankind in a new way, and so in a real sense altered His active relationship to men; manifestation of what human selfishness means for divine love rendered morally appropriate a new method of action on the part of the divine love. But the love itself was unchanged.

July Thirteenth

584. PROFIT MOTIVE

So long as we rely on the Profit-motive (as distinct from a secure but limited return on capital invested) as the mainspring of production, so long we shall be in a condition always verging towards faction within and war without.

585. CONTROL BY FINANCE

Finance may rightly exercise a check, calling a halt to avoid bankruptcy; but for positive control it is functionally unfitted. Yet it exercises such control to a very large extent.

586. GOSPEL AND ECONOMIC SYSTEM

There may be complete disagreement as to whether you would bring about a juster state of affairs by nationalisation of the means of production, distribution and exchange. You may think that would be the best way; but there are many who are persuaded that exactly the poorest people would then be less fortunate than now, because having removed the profit motive of the existing economic system, you would introduce a greater measure of inefficiency, and it would be the weakest who would suffer most. We must form what opinion we think right about it—a perfectly good Christian may hold either view. There is nothing in the Gospel to say what is to be held as to the economic system.

July Fourteenth

587. DIVINE COMMUNITY

From the dawn of history, even from that twilight where history, legend and myth are inextricably intermingled, there had been a community conscious of divine commission. Its origin is recorded in the Call of Abraham, in whom all families of the earth should be blessed (Genesis xii. 1-3). If this story represents rather a tribal migration than an individual adventure, as some scholars think, that sharpens the point of our contention. When history begins, the commissioned community already exists.

588. BOND OF DISCIPLES

"That ye love one another as I loved you." . . . Love to the point of sacrifice even of life, is to be the bond between His disciples. This is not a command to all the world; nor is it a command concerning the relation of Christians to non-Christians. It is the command to the Christian fellowship.

589. EARTHLY FELLOWSHIP

Is our fellowship in Christ a reality more profound and effective than our membership of our earthly fellowships—family, school, party, class, nation, race—and able in consequence to unite us in love across all natural divisions and hostilities? Of course not. And the reason is that we do not truly abide in Him.

July Fifteenth

590. KINDS OF EVIL

Evil is of three main kinds—Error, Suffering and Sin, and to a very great extent the two former are due to the last.

591. SPIRITUAL PRIDE

A demon of spiritual pride, which most of us are not nearly good enough even to encounter, the saints assure us, is waiting as it were on the top rung of the ladder of perfection to catch us even there and throw us down. . . . It is not merely pride in being good; it is pride in being delivered from pride; it is pride in being humble. It turns even self-sacrifice into a form of self-assertion.

592. ORIGINAL SIN

I suggest that what we mean by freedom as applied to the human will is the capacity to do what seems to us good, and the trouble is that what seems to us good is not at first, or by nature, what really is good. We start, so to speak, with a handicap. It is in our nature; it is original. And the great myth with which the Bible opens sets the whole thing very vividly before us. It is by attaining to knowledge of good and evil that man involves himself also in the entanglement of sin.

July Sixteenth

593. THE PRE-EXISTENT CHURCH

The Church is the Body of Christ. Yet the writers of the New Testament never regard it as coming into existence at the Nativity— still less as being born or inaugurated at the Feast of Pentecost. It was there before Christ came to redeem it.

594. EXTENSION OF INCARNATION

It is the whole meaning of the Church as His Body that His Divine Spirit should, by subduing our selfish wills and binding us into the unity of love, declare His nature and fulfil His purpose through the ages and across the world, as that nature was declared and that purpose fulfilled in Palestine by means of the Body born of Mary.

595. CHURCH PROPERTY

If it is desirable to nationalise certain forms of property, such as minerals, the Church has no claim to treatment in its capacity as an owner which differentiates it from other owners. For the Church in its true nature has no concern with such things; its property is an instrument for the doing of its work.

July Seventeenth

596. EUCHARISTIC SACRIFICE: MY BODY

How would the disciples think of those strange words, "This is my Body"? Inevitably they would see that as in that moment He treated the bread, so in that moment He was treating His Body: "He brake it and gave it." He was offering a sacrifice; the victim was Himself.

597. DEVOTIONAL LANGUAGE

Great damage is done to the cause of true religion when the great phrases of devotion are either treated as scientific definitions from which inferences may be drawn by a rigid deduction . . . or else are dismissed as meaningless because they have a poetic and not a scientific meaning.

142

598. Eucharistic Memorial

At the Eucharist we, being gathered together before God, make remembrance of the sacrifice of Christ by repeating the very act with which He accompanied and interpreted His spiritual offering of it.

July Eighteenth

599. "Come, Holy Ghost"

When we pray, "Come, Holy Ghost, our souls inspire," we had better know what we are about. He will not carry us to easy triumphs and gratifying successes; more probably He will set us to some task for God in the full intention that we shall fail, so that others, learning wisdom by our failure, may carry the good cause forward.

600. Real Dignity

If we invoke the Holy Spirit, we must be ready for the glorious pain of being caught by His power out of our petty orbit into the eternal purposes of the Almighty, in whose onward sweep our loves are as a speck of dust. The soul that is filled with the Spirit must have become purged of all pride or love of ease, all self-complacence and self-reliance; but that soul has found the only real dignity, the only lasting joy. Come then, Great Spirit, come. Convict the world; and convict my timid soul.

601. Falling into Sin

We all know with what fatal ease we accept a position prepared for us if it is presented suddenly and offers a refuge from many troubles. And then the harm is done! The act seemed so nearly innocent; the avoidance of its guilty consequence is so very hard.

July Nineteenth

602. Family Membership

Membership of family and nation is not an accidental appendage of my individuality, but a constitutive element in it. It is always vain to say, "If I had been a son of Napoleon Bonaparte," or any such thing. I *am* the son of my own father, and if he had had no son, but Napoleon had had an additional one, that means that someone else would have been born instead of me.

603. MAN SOCIAL FROM BIRTH

A man's relation to his parents is not accidental; he is in the heart of his being their child. We are social through and through; it is thus that God has made us, and our self-centredness is an offence not only against Him and our neighbours, but against our own real nature.

604. UNDERSTANDING OTHER DENOMINATIONS

When we meet a fellow Christian with whom we disagree, we are less inclined than formerly to be sure he must be merely wrong. Perhaps he has seen something that we have missed. Anyhow, no man falls into an error which has no attractiveness. At least let us first learn what he fears that he may lose by accepting our interpretation in place of his own.

July Twentieth

605. POLITICAL TEST

Man is created for fellowship in the family of God: fellowship first with God, and through that with all God's other children. And that is the primary test that must be applied to every system that is constructed and every change in the system that is proposed.

606. MAJORITY GOVERNMENT

The defence of government by a majority is not that the majority is always right; on the contrary, the only thing you know for certain about a majority with regard to any new issue is that it's sure to be a little wrong. Only you have no earthly means of finding out which of the minorities, if any, is right; and it is very unlikely that the majority will be as wrong as some of the minorities are likely to be. Therefore it is a great deal safer to let the majority rule than a minority.

607. HERD AND FELLOWSHIP

The real defence of democracy is . . . that by calling upon people to exercise responsible judgment on the matters before the country at any time, you develop their personal qualities: you make them feel that they belong to one another in this corporate society, and so you tend to deepen and intensify personal fellowship. You are leading people forward from the relationship of the herd to that of real fellowship by the mere process of calling upon them to take their share in the government of the groups of which they are members.

July Twenty-first

608. USES OF SUFFERING

Suffering is the indispensable condition of fortitude, and it is the most potent stimulus and bond of sympathy. Perhaps if we were not so self-centred we should find in *joy* as strong a stimulus to sympathy as in pain or sorrow; it is certain that in fact we do not find it so.

609. ANIMAL SUFFERING

If indeed there be close continuity between the evolutionary stages, it may be possible to show that the conditions which involve animal suffering are those which also at the human level give occasion for such virtues as fortitude, so that the justification of human suffering may be held to cover also by implication the suffering of animals.

610. LUNACY

It is perhaps one of the consolations in face of the bewildering problem of some kinds of lunacy to reflect that lunacy at least often (I do not at all suppose always) represents an internal tension between good and evil which had become unbearable. But if so, it means that the good is still struggling, and in the light of eternity there is hope.

July Twenty-second

611. OTHER MINISTRIES

Are we entitled to say of any ministry transmitted by other than the channels familiar for centuries to the whole Church, that they have been "blessed and owned by the Holy Spirit" and are "within their several spheres real ministries in the Universal Church"? I cannot doubt that we are both entitled and obliged to make such a judgment. And if we thus judge that the Holy Spirit has blessed and owned these ministries, can we without presumption and profanity refuse to recognise them ourselves?

612. RECOGNISING IRREGULAR MINISTRIES

We cannot in practice recognise what we must regard as irregular ministries, however effective within their own spheres, until there is an operative decision to unite in a way that ends the irregularity. But when that is present, ought we not to be ready to recognise during a period of transition what God has blessed and owned until the new rule is generally established and all ministers have been episcopally ordained?

613. REUNION

The way to the union of Christendom does not lie through committee-rooms, though there is a task of formulation to be done there. It lies through personal union with the Lord so deep and real as to be comparable with His union with the Father.

July Twenty-third

614. IMMORTALITY ONLY PARTLY RELIGIOUS

If God is righteous—still more, if God is Love—immortality follows as a consequence. He made me; He loves me; He will not let me perish, so long as there is in me anything that He can love. And that is a wholesome reflection for me if, but only if, the result is that I give greater glory to God in the first place and take comfort to myself only, if at all, in the second place. I wish to stress this heavily. *Except as an implicate in the righteousness and love of God, immortality is not a religious interest at all.*

615. IMMORTALITY ON GOD'S TERMS

Man is not immortal by nature or of right; but he is capable of immortality and there is offered to him resurrection from the dead and life eternal if he will receive it from God and on God's terms. There is nothing arbitrary in that offer or in those terms, for God is perfect Wisdom and perfect Love.

616. IMMORTALITY AS FOOD FOR SELF-CENTREDNESS

If my desire is first for future life for myself, or even first for reunion with those whom I have loved and lost, then the doctrine of immortality may do me positive harm by fixing me in that self-concern or in concern for my own joy in my friends. But if my desire is first for God's glory, and for myself that I may be used to promote it, then the doctrine of immortality will give me new heart in the assurance that what here must be a very imperfect service may be made perfect hereafter.

July Twenty-fourth

617. EVANGELISM

It is the manifestation of God's love toward us in our mutual love which shall at last convert the world.

618. HATING CHRIST'S CALL

We shall not, perhaps, ever allow ourselves to hate Christ and His Cross as historically presented; we very easily hate His call to the Cross when it comes to ourselves to-day.

619. BEING A CHRISTIAN

It is quite easy to be a genial libertine—friendly with everyone you meet, if you have for yourself and them no moral standard. And it is fairly easy for you to set up a moral standard for yourself and others—no doubt underlining the words *"for others"*—if you allow yourself in the process to become hypercritical, unsympathetic and censorious, which is to be a Pharisee. But to set up a standard for others and yourself—with the words *"for yourself"* underlined—and still show sympathy and love to those who fail to reach it, without letting the standard down, that is very hard. But that is to be a Christian.

July Twenty-fifth

620. IDLENESS AND THEFT

Every man is a consumer, whether he is also a producer or not; that is why idleness and theft are morally indistinguishable. The idle man (however much he legally possesses) is consuming without producing; he enjoys what he does not earn.

621. SAFETY FIRST

When people invite you to take a safe course they always mean the same thing—that you should select some disaster which is not the worst possible and involve yourself in it. Thus you have safety against the worst which might otherwise befall you. But you can only play for safety by repudiation of the ideal. The pursuit of the ideal is always fraught with peril.

622. Reduced Standards of Living

The more fortunate sections of our country, probably including some grades of labour, must be ready to accept a reduced standard of living, so that the good things of the earth may be more equitably shared both between the nations and within the nations.

July Twenty-sixth

623. Christians in Politics

Suppose a man feels convinced that he can do a great deal of good for the country as a party politician, and yet knows that, in order to be effective as a member of either party, he will have to put in his pocket a certain number of convictions, at any rate for a time: well, it seems to me quite clear that it is his duty to do it. . . . It is unquestionably desirable that a man with high Christian ideals should be willing to take part in that political life, even on such terms, rather than leave the national politics in the hands of people who have got no such ideals, which is the actual alternative.

624. Clergy and Politics

The Church and the official representatives of the Church must keep themselves free from the entanglements of party politics. There will come times when they should support or resist a specific measure; but they should not take any share in the strife of parties. Their business is something far more fundamental and important; it is the formation of that mind and temper in the whole community which will lead to wholesome legislation by any party and all parties.

625. Planning and Freedom

The chief enemy of freedom to-day is not an intelligent plan but the irresistible pressure of blind forces. We must gain control of those forces, and that involves planning.

July Twenty-seventh

626. THE SPIRIT AND FACTS

Occasional words and acts display the spirit in its living relation to the facts confronting it; and it is the spirit that is universal in its scope, it is the spirit that is entitled to authority; and its authority can only be recognised by a private act of judgment.

627. JESUS AND COERCION

They *went back and walked no more with him*; and He let them go. As He will not coerce us into His companionship, so He will not hold us there against our will.

628. PRIVATE JUDGMENT

The spiritual authority of the Gospel for those who accept it is secured by the fact that it is transmitted in a form which perpetually calls for private judgment.

July Twenty-eighth

629. INTERNATIONAL SOLICITATION

It has been a conspicuous vice of recent political thought and action to suppose that no nation is interested in the internal affairs of another.

630. NAZI PHILOSOPHY

Some of our politicians and diplomatists have suggested that it was necessary, before May 15, 1939, to watch and see whether the Nazis would apply to other States the principles on which they had seized and maintained power over their own fellow citizens. That is a false suggestion. The only real question was not whether they would do this, but when.

631. ESTABLISHMENT

The only sound form of "Establishment"—not a control of religion by the State, but an agreement on the part of the State to recognise the divine authority of the Church and to lend its aid in the upholding of the order of the Church so far as this may be required by the Church itself.

July Twenty-ninth

632. THE PEACE OF GOD

What would give meaning to all the movement of History is the attainment of that synoptic vision of its process which at once appreciates the process as such and yet enables the mind to compass it instead of being immersed in it. Such a serene relationship to the occurrences of Time . . . is perhaps one part of what has been called the Peace of God.

633. DRAMATIC UNITY

The historical order together with the climax which is a transition to something more and other than history is one of those unities where the principle of unity is in the whole, so that even what precedes is fully intelligible only when what follows has completely developed the ground of the necessity of every part. This type of unity, as we have seen, is perfectly familiar in every good poem or drama.

634. HISTORY PARTISANS

Now, myself, I like historians to be strong partisans. I like to read, for example, the history of our Civil War written by a strong Royalist, and by a strong Republican, first one and then the other, and then make up my own mind. I don't want him to pretend to be impartial, because I know he is not.

July Thirtieth

635. VARIATION IN LOVE

An earthly father who loves all his children equally may yet have special ties of intimacy with each one, a peculiar tenderness in every case; this one is so eager, that one so gentle, another so wistfully affectionate; he does not love one more than another, but he loves each differently. It makes the love of God seem less remote in its holiness when we learn that it contains within itself a similar variation of individual attachment.

636. HUMILITY AND HONOUR

Humility, whatever else it may involve, is primarily forgetfulness of self. Now a man who has forgotten himself, if he has got a great work to do, will not be lacking in force. On the contrary, he will fling himself into the work with an abandonment quite unknown to the man who is self-conscious. He ignores insults, because he does not know he is insulted; he is unencumbered by the ridiculous appendage which military people call their honour.

637. STRENGTH THROUGH PRAYER
We human beings are selfish folk; and when we are tired we tend to be more selfish than ever. We shall not find strength in ourselves to dedicate our lives with the completeness which is demanded; we must seek it in our prayers.

July Thirty-first

638. CHRIST AND LIFE OF CHURCH
I am convinced that our Lord rejected the apocalyptic form of the Messianic hope as completely as the political-prophetic form. I am totally unimpressed by the argument that He did not expect any long life for His Church on earth.

639. BEGOTTEN SON
The Son is in all ways derivative and dependent—"begotten." But though in this way He is "subordinate," the range of His derived activity is coextensive with the Father's. He can do nothing of Himself, but He does all that the Father does. He is agent, not principal; but He is universal agent.

640. DEATH WAS VICTORY
That His body should die was no defeat; defeat for Him must have taken the form of cursing His enemies or sinking into self-concern. But through all the anguish love was serenely unshaken. To die thus was, in and for His own person, to conquer hate.

151

AUGUST

August First

641. CALVARY

Here, in this life of perfect obedience and love; here, in this courage that bears the worst that hate can do and is still unfalteringly calm; here, in this love that is unquenched and undiminished by the desertion of friends, by the blows and jeers of enemies—here we see Man fulfilling his true destiny and manifested as superior to circumstance.

642. BEYOND THE SACRAMENTS

The Sacraments of the Church are appointed means of grace wherein the Lord of the Church makes use, for His central purpose, of the character implanted by Him in the constitution of the universe as a whole. They represent and focus a principle at work far beyond themselves.

643. CHRIST'S HUMANITY

The human nature of Christ conceals the Deity from us, as it did from the Jews, until we are united with it and find the Deity indwelling it. We must *eat the flesh of the Son of Man and drink His blood* (John vi. 53) so that His humanity becomes the substance of our very being.

August Second

644. REVELATION IN NATURE AND CONSCIENCE

The revelation given in the majesty of the starry heavens may be perfect in its kind, though its kind is markedly inadequate; the revelation given through the reason and conscience of man is more adequate in kind, but in that kind is usually imperfect.

645. FATHERHOOD OF GOD

Christ does not reveal all that is meant by the word God. There ever remains the unsearchable abyss of Deity. But He reveals what it vitally concerns us to know; He reveals God as Father.

646. Locus of Revelation

The typical locus of revelation is not the mind of the seer but the historical event. And if the revelation is essentially an event or fact, then it can be perfectly definite, although it neither is nor can be exhaustively represented in propositions. Moreover, it can be a focus of unity for people whose interpretation of it is various.

August Third

647. Kingdom of God in This World

The Christian religion gives us no assurance that there will ever be upon this earth a society of perfect love, indeed it gives us many reasons to believe there never will be, but it is a matter of small consequence whether the divine purpose to sum up all things in Christ be fulfilled on this planet or not. Certainly it cannot be completely fulfilled on this planet, because there will always be born into this world new finite spirits who take themselves to be the centre of the world and so upset all the harmony again.

648. Creation and Redemption

We must ever keep in mind the two thoughts—God the Creator of the universe, which came into being at His word; God the Redeemer staggering beneath a load that crushes Him as He goes from Jerusalem to Calvary: so far harder is it to redeem men from selfishness to love than to create the wheeling systems of the stars.

649. Love's Earthly Disclosure

The perfect love of the Father for the Son and of the Son for the Father—which is the Holy Spirit—is the glory of the Godhead. It is eternal. In the earthly sojourn of the Son it is historically disclosed; but itself it is eternal.

August Fourth

650. Sermons

The sermons for which we are most grateful are those which help us to believe vitally what we knew quite well before the sermon started.

651. QUARRELSOME CONGREGATIONS

If congregations are quarrelsome or self-complacent, no amount of preaching can counteract the harm that is done.

652. CYNICISM AND FALSE PIETY

Worldly cynicism is less nauseating than pious humbug! The course of honest testimony to principle in this tangled world is very difficult and only possible where faith in God has really exorcised self-centredness and self-concern.

August Fifth

653. SELFISHNESS IN PRAYER

We must begin with prayer, because if you are selfish in your prayers there is not much hope that you will be really unselfish anywhere else.

654. LORD'S PRAYER

I wonder where most of you begin to mean business as you say the Lord's Prayer. . . . Our Lord says that when you come into the presence of God you should forget all about yourself and your needs, even your sins; you should be so filled with the thought of God that what you want above all things is that God's Name may be hallowed—reverenced—throughout the world. You are to ask for that first, because you ought to want it most. And next, that He may be effectively King of the world He has made, so that all men obey His law; and then, that His whole purpose of love shall be carried out unspoiled by the selfishness of men.

655. A MIND IN TUNE

What does your mind run on when there is no reason why it should run on anything? What does it turn to spontaneously when you wake in the morning? It must be in tune with Christ.

August Sixth

656. THE TRANSFIGURATION

In the ecstasy of the Transfiguration the theme of discourse between the Head of the Law, the Head of the Prophets and the Head of the New Order is the Exodus which He will accomplish at Jerusalem; the word Exodus carries a double meaning—for Him decease, for His people deliverance.

657. AFTER THE TRANSFIGURATION

On the journey to Jerusalem, as the Messiah marches on His capital, two disciples ask if they may be specially near Him in His glory. His answer is "Can you share My sacrifice?"—for the sacrifice *is* the glory.

658. DIVINITY OF CHRIST

Most of us are not able to attribute any such meaning to the word "Divine" as will enable us to use that word of Christ, unless we have first seen God in Christ Himself. To ask whether Christ is divine is to suggest that Christ is an enigma while Deity is a simple and familiar conception. But the truth is the exact opposite.

August Seventh

659. THE WORLD JUDGED

The world thought that it was judging Christ when Caiaphas rent his clothes, and the people shouted, "He is worthy of death," and Pilate gave sentence as they desired. But we know that it was they, and not He, upon whom sentence was then passed.

660. "SECOND" COMING

Our answer to the apocalyptic critics of the day will be to say: Yes, surely Christ did expect His coming almost immediately; but it was not a *second* coming. There is nothing in His own language about a second coming. That all arises from the disciples' failure to rise to the full height of His teaching. He speaks of the Coming of the Son of Man.

661. CHRIST'S SAYINGS

How can I in practice, ask in Christ's name or as His representative? Only if I am abiding in Him and His *sayings* abide in me. It is through His sayings that this mutual indwelling is effected. We do well to remember that our Lord is much more than a teacher. But a teacher He is; and it is through His teaching that our minds receive His mind so that we may become one with Him and He with us.

August Eighth

662. CHRISTIAN FELLOWSHIP

Let us become conscious of ourselves as a fellowship pledged to God and to one another to stand and contend for international and social justice; to set little store by our possessions and much by our responsibilities; to seek, in worship, at once the understanding of our task and the quality by which we may perform it; to make use of the service appointed by our Lord as the symbol of our social life and the means of our personal dedication; and daily to commit ourselves, our country and all mankind to God in the prayer our Lord has taught us.

663. SPENDING

It would be very rash to say there is any section of English society of which the spontaneously accepted standard of reference is identical with the mind of Christ. We must therefore perpetually criticise these accepted standards and the promptings in our own souls with reference to the mind of Christ, and find out how far it is really justifiable to go in that way—whether, for example, the kind of expenditure upon pleasure which we find to be quite normal among our friends and acquaintances really represents the mind of Christ.

664. CIRCUMFERENCES OF LOYALTY

A man must in practice serve his family, his city, his firm, his trade union or what not; the overriding obligation to the entire spiritual fellowship can in practice only be expressed through the prohibition of any service to the narrower unit or structure which involves injury to the wider.

August Ninth

665. SCHISM AND APOSTASY

Schism is undoubtedly a sinful state, being contrary to the declared purpose of God, yet schism is within the Church, the Body of Christ, and does not effect separation from it as do apostasy and infidelity.

666. GUILT OF SCHISM

Sinful as schism is, there is no guilt of schism in those who are loyal to the teaching which they have received, still less in those who have been converted from heathenism by missionaries of one or another of our sadly manifold traditions. It is one of the greatest evils of our divisions that they are reproduced in the experience of converts who have no responsibility for them.

667. THE AGENT OF GOD'S PURPOSE

The purpose of God in creation was, and is, to fashion a fellowship of free spirits knit together by a love in all its members which answers to the manifested love of God. . . . The agent of that purpose is the Church, which is therefore called the Body of Christ.

August Tenth

668. THE NEW CRITERION OF GREATNESS

The Christian conception of God begins with an exaltation of the Divine Majesty, the greatest the mind can conceive, but when the greatness and the far-reaching power, might and authority of God exhibit themselves for man, it is by washing the disciples' feet.

669. CONSTANCY OF PURPOSE

There is nothing majestic about invariable constancy of personal action, which remains unaltered whether the circumstances are the same or not; rather should it be called mulish. Constancy of purpose is a noble characteristic, but it shows itself, not in unalterable uniformity of conduct, but in perpetual self-adaptation, with an infinite delicacy of graduation, to different circumstances, so that, however these may vary, the one unchanging purpose is always served.

670. ETERNAL SIGNIFICANCE OF MORAL BEHAVIOUR

The spiritual richness of God's eternal being is in some measure constituted by the moral achievements of His temporal creatures.

August Eleventh

671. BORROWING CREDIT

To me it seems ridiculous, when the nation needs credit for the carrying-out of its own purposes, that it should borrow that credit from a section of itself and pay interest on it. The source out of which repayment has to come is of course the whole national production. That is the real security, and I cannot see why anything more should be paid for it than the actual administrative cost, which a very high authority has told me is perhaps one-eighth of one per cent.

672. DISESTABLISHMENT

I cannot see that the question of Establishment is any direct concern of the Church as such at all. It is the concern of the State; and it is a concern for us as Christian citizens influencing the State; and I believe there are values connected with Establishment for the life of the nation and State which would be lost by Disestablishment, and which would be hard to replace. But it is no concern of the Church. We have a divine commission; we exist as a divine creation. If the earthly State likes to associate itself with us, let it.

673. PERMANENT PENALTIES

So far as any settlement is penal it loses its quality of justice as the years pass. No penal settlement can be both just and permanent, for you must not personify a nation and treat it as though it were a single moral agent. It consists of a multitude of individuals, and these are grouped in successive generations.

August Twelfth

674. MORAL GROWTH

A system of rewards and penalties may have a disciplinary use in fashioning the will, by holding in check certain lawless impulses and thus allowing an opportunity for the dominant nucleus to establish itself and become a rudimentary will. And thereafter this will may itself direct conduct in accordance with right moral principles because it is itself concerned with the winning of rewards or the avoidance of penalties. But in such a case the will is not really directed to moral principle; it is directed to pleasure and pain.

675. FAILURE IN DUTY

Other men find in a failure of duty a breach of moral law, an offence against society, a disgrace to self; the religious man finds there disloyalty to a king, betrayal of a friend.

676. MAKING DECISIONS

The greatest decisions always have to be taken before there is a complete sufficiency of evidence, because it is only after they have been made, and the experiment tried out, that the evidence can be there.

August Thirteenth

677. NEWS ABOUT GOD

The religious value of the doctrine of the Incarnation is not found in what it affirms concerning the historical Figure, Jesus of Nazareth, but in what it affirms concerning the eternal God.

678. THE KINGDOM'S CONTROL

It is not the difference of the super-natural from the natural that distinguishes Christ's Kingdom; it is the difference between control of conduct by force and control of heart and mind and will by love and truth.

679. DIVINE JUDGMENT

We tend to think of the Divine Judgment as being the infliction upon us by an irresistible Despot of penalties, not growing out of our characters and deeds, but imposed from without. . . . The Divine Judgment is the verdict upon us which consists in our reaction to *the light* when it is offered to us.

August Fourteenth

680. CHURCH AND POLITICS

We must begin to organise our industry with the supply of need as the primary aim and the making of profits as entirely incidental. This is a return to the "natural order" as it exists in the mind of the Creator, but of course it is a reversal of the order natural to the selfishness of men! The Church cannot say how it is to be done; but it is called to say that it must be done, and to demand of those upon whom the change will impose sacrifices that they accept these with goodwill in the name of fellowship and service.

There the Church stops, and the State, moved by its citizens and by the Christian impulse communicated through them from the Church, takes up the task. There is room here for abundance of divergent opinions.

681. Equality and Democracy

It is perfectly compatible with Equality rightly understood that some should command and some should obey, and all that we need to purge such a view of all that may make it embittering is to recognise that to obey is quite as noble as to command.

682. Private Enterprise

I would advocate a vast extension of public control of private enterprise; especially I would advocate a wide extension of the limitation of profits wherever liability is limited—a model scheme could be found before the war in the great glass-works at Jena.

August Fifteenth

683. Religious Experience in History

The statement, "To you is born a Saviour which is Christ the Lord," uses categories of which history knows nothing; yet if it is true at all, it is historically true.

684. National Self-sacrifice

The Christian nation will, I think, be prepared to defend by force others who are being oppressed; but, so far as its own interest is concerned, it will choose rather to perish than to stain its soul by the passion of war. Nor do I believe that, until some nation has done this, there will be any hope of international civilisation. Of course such a choice must be the act of the whole people and not of a government resting on a precarious majority; and, until the nation is prepared for such an act of self-sacrifice, wars of self-defence are inevitable, and in that sense justified so far as concerns those who technically declare them and those who fight in them.

685. The Temptations

Immediately after the baptism He goes out into the wilderness to face temptations, some at least of which arise from the previous conceptions of the Messiahship. First there is the temptation, which arises simply from His human nature, to use the power that belongs to Him as Messiah for His own convenience. . . . We find our Lord next meditating political methods, looking out over the kingdoms of the earth and the glory of them, and yearning for them for the Kingdom of God. . . . Then comes the severest of all. . . . It is the temptation to fulfil the apocalyptic expectation and to appear descending upon Jerusalem upborne by angels; but it is a satire, for after all He would not be descending from heaven, but falling from the Temple pinnacle.

August Sixteenth

686. Reference to the Mind of Christ

Christianity offers no picture of the goal of social life. It is true that we know not whither He is leading us; in answer to the question, "We know not whither Thou goest; how can we know the way?" the answer is, "I am the way." And that way always starts from where we are. There is no circumstance in life in which it is not possible for us to consider what is the mind of Christ and conform our own thought and conduct to it.

687. The Function of Creeds

We cannot too often insist upon this point, that the centre of Christian faith is not an intellectual proposition, but a person, and the value of all the intellectual propositions and all the formulations of theology is that they give us guidance, resting upon the experience of multitudes of Christians, by which we may enter into that same relationship to Christ which those multitudes of Christians have already enjoyed.

688. Credal Affirmation

We affirm our faith in the Creed which should always be a confession of the trust we already have in God and an aspiration towards the deeper trust which we need.

August Seventeenth

689. VARIETIES OF CHRISTIAN EXPERIENCE

The full Christian life cannot be lived only in groups of like-minded Christians; for if they are like-minded they merely strengthen one another in those elements of Christian and faith experience in which they are already fairly strong.

690. BISHOP—DEFECTIVE COMMISSION

Where any great part of the Church refuses to recognise a bishop or the commission bestowed through him, the commission is to that extent defective, not in authority (which comes from Christ alone), but in effectiveness.

691. ORGANS OF UNIVERSAL CHURCH

To me it would seem shocking presumption to question the reality of the Sacraments administered, for example, in the Presbyterian Church of Scotland or the Lutheran Church of Germany. As Christian disciples, the members of those bodies belong to the soul of the Catholic Church; by baptism they are admitted to membership in its body. But it is not only as individuals that they form part of the Catholic Church. These bodies themselves are not mere religious societies, of which the several members are, by virtue of their faith and baptism, members of the Universal Church. They are, as their fruits have shown, parts and organs of the Universal Church.

August Eighteenth

692. THE LEAVEN OF THE EARLY CHURCH

He prepared His disciples for a change after the critical moment was passed; with the Cross and Resurrection His Kingdom would have come with power, and they were no longer to be apart from the world, bringing to it *ab extra* the divine act of redemption which is itself the revelation of God, but were to carry its power into the world as leaven that should leaven the whole lump.

693. THE CONTROL OF CONDUCT

There are three ways, and the only three ways, in which the conduct of men can be controlled without winning their loyalty. Bribery, appealing to their natural desires; force, which secures obedience by making it not worth while to disobey; and over-whelming evidence which affords such demonstration of the claim presented that it becomes foolishness to resist it. Those are the three things which in the wilderness He considered and turned down; and what form of the Messianic expectation has He left? He left nothing. . . . He goes forth among men living the life of perfect love.

694. Love Expressed in Sacrifice

The Son of Man must suffer because sacrifice is the real expression of love; and God, whose Kingdom He came to found, is first and foremost a God of Love, and the response He seeks is the response that loving hearts give to love which has shown itself in sacrifice for them.

August Nineteenth

695. Prayer Book Language

There is often complaint that the Prayer Book services are too difficult in their language. It is not so much the language that is difficult as the ideas which it expresses, the Christian conceptions which are not understood even by many Christians and which are altogether foreign to those outside.

696. Self in Mercy

Whereas mercifulness or forgiveness is almost an insult when offered to us by a man who is conscious of his own virtue, every taint of that is removed when there is no trace of self at all in his action. It is the self in his mercy that is annoying.

697. Composing a Quarrel

If a man should go to two people who are quarrelling and offer to make peace between them, it would certainly seem officious and interfering if it was felt he was thinking of himself or of his duty in doing it; but if he made peace by the mere fact that in his presence quarrelling became difficult or impossible there could be no offence.

August Twentieth

698. AUTHORITY—A RATIONAL PRINCIPLE

At first all faith rests upon authority. No doubt the authority to which a child, for example, gives his trust is not that of the apostles, but of his parents and teachers. It is because of what they tell him that he reads with reverent mind the writings of the apostles. But it is always first on authority. Authority is not something irrational. So far as it becomes irrational it ceases to be authority at all and becomes compulsion. Authority, if the word is properly used, is a strictly rational principle.

699. BELIEF AND AUTHORITY

In many activities of life we have to act according to knowledge which we have not acquired for ourselves—the specialist knowledge of the physician and the lawyer, for example. We accept their authority and act by it. When we discover, through any researches of our own, the ground for the advice that they have given, then we have an added reason, but not for the first time reason at all, for the beliefs that we hold and the practice that follows upon them.

700. PROOF AND BELIEF

We all know people who tell us they cannot believe what cannot be proved. Of course it is not true. Of course they do in fact believe a great deal that they cannot prove—concerning the trustworthiness of their friends, for example.

August Twenty-first

701. MINISTERIAL INSTRUMENT OF CHRIST

When I consecrate a godly and well-learned man to the office and work of a Bishop in the Church of God, I do not act as a representative of the Church, if by that is meant the whole number of contemporary Christians; but I do act as the ministerial instrument of Christ in His Body, the Church.

702. NOT BORN FREE

Freedom, so far as it is of actual value, is not something native to men; we are not born free; we have to win freedom. Not only so—for we find that we cannot in fact win true freedom; we can only receive it. We do not make ourselves free; the truth, when we know it, makes us free.

703. GOAL OF FREEDOM

To try to maintain an abstract freedom with no determinate goal is to court disaster. Freedom is not only freedom from something, but freedom for something.

August Twenty-second

704. "BECOMING INTEGRATED"

I find great occasion for alarm in very much of that modern practice of psychotherapy from which no doubt we are also going to gain great benefits. But in some of this practice there is a strong suggestion that all we have to do is somehow to become at peace with ourselves, to restore an internal harmony, to become, as they like to say, fully integrated. And I want to ask, about what centre?—with what manner of self is my whole being to be harmonised?

705. REDEMPTION THROUGH LOVE

How can the self find it good to submit willingly to removal from its self-centredness and welcome reconstruction about God as centre? There is in fact one power known to men, and only one, which can effect this, not only for one or another function of the self (as beauty and truth can do) but for the self as a whole in its entirety and integrity. When a man acts to please one whom he loves, doing or bearing what apart from that love he would not choose to do or bear, his action is wholly determined by the other's pleasure, yet in no action is he so utterly free—that is, so utterly determined by his apparent good.

706. DEALING WITH TEMPTATIONS

Sometimes it is possible to change the apparent good by setting beside it some presentation of the real good. There are many who habitually gain control of evil desires by turning their attention to the Figure of Christ, in contrast with which the object of the evil desire appears no longer good but abhorrent.

August Twenty-third

707. CHRISTIAN SOCIETY

We may be Christian Englishmen, but then at the best we are only English Christians, and we are only as Christian as the influence of England will let us be. Consequently, we are bound to secure that the society in which we live shall itself become as Christian in all its institutions as it can be made.

708. OUR SIN

If you take some millions of people just like ourselves, generous up to a point but still predominantly selfish, with varying abilities, and leave them to live together for several generations, the result will be something like the horror of our present European civilisation. The sin that has made it is just our sin.

709. CLERGY AND ECONOMICS

No degree of personal piety and no amount of theological learning will enable a man in the smallest degree to pronounce a competent judgment upon the probable actual effects of any economic action.

August Twenty-fourth

710. GOD AND "THE ALL"

God is not the totality of things—the All; nor is He an immanent principle to which all things conform; He is Spirit—active energy, alive and purposive, but free from the temporal and spatial limitations which are characteristic of matter.

711. DIVINE SELF-EXPRESSION

If God is Personal, He must express Himself; the Word was in the beginning with God; but His self-expression is not the self expressed; that remains always cause, never effect.

712. DIVINE AUTHORITY

When God speaks to either the heart or the conscience He does not first prove His right to do so. The divine command is its own evidence, and the heart or conscience that is not utterly numbed by complacent sin recognises its inherent authority.

August Twenty-fifth

713. The Business of Church and State

The reason for having different rules is not that the Church and the State are concerned to uphold different moralities, but that they discharge different functions in relation to the one morality. The business of the State surely is to get the best possible results out of a given material so far as human foresight can anticipate the consequences of any action. The business of the Church is to uphold an ideal. The value of the ideal is quite independent of the question whether, at the moment, anyone is realising it.

714. Intellectual Leadership

If the Church is to hold respect and bring a helpful influence, it must in its own corporate life show its educational excellence: and it is there that it must regain what it has too much lost, the intellectual leadership of our people.

715. Being Christians

Our action is all response; all initiative is with the Lord. . . . Those of us who were baptised as infants are without excuse if we forget this. Our being Christians is no doing of ours, any more than our being civilised; it is something done to us and for us, not by us, though we have to make appropriate response in the form of obedience prompted by love.

August Twenty-sixth

716. History

Science, art and morals are all involved in the study of history.

717. Self-centredness

We cannot go behind the Reformation—that great *bouleversement* of human thinking, wherein it was for the first time fully recognised that each man is by nature the centre of his own universe, however true it be that his most urgent need is to discover that it does not revolve about him as its pivot.

718. History: Its Goal

The meaning of history is found in the development of an ever wider fellowship of ever richer personalities. The goal of history, in short, is the Commonwealth of Value.

August Twenty-seventh

719. LOVE, NOT VIRTUE

In all my strivings to attain some ideal or perform some service, unless my heart and will are wholly captivated, there will be some self-assertion, and probably a great deal. That is why the consciously virtuous person is disagreeable. It is not virtue that can save the world or anyone in it, but love. And love is not at our command. We cannot generate it from within ourselves. We can win it only by surrender to it.

720. INCOMPLETE SURRENDER

So far as it is to the Divine Self-Utterance or Word in truth or beauty or goodness that men open their hearts, their works are done through "the grace of Jesus Christ and the Inspiration of His Spirit." That may be a real surrender, but not complete; therefore those works, while not mere sins, yet have some of "the nature of sin" about them.

721. GOD'S WORD

The Word of God is not a passive principle of rational unity but an active force of moral judgment.

August Twenty-eighth

722. UTILITARIANISM

As selfishness learns by experience it attains to prudence, and those who zealously follow the best policy will about as often as not be honest. Outward morality is thus encouraged even by the immoral principle itself. . . . Some genuine progress is thus made; but to an almost equal extent conscience is confused and the edge of its witness blunted.

723. WEALTH

We have not driven home upon men His clear intuition that though, if wealth comes, it ought to be accepted and used as an opportunity, yet it must be recognised as rather a snare to the spiritual life than an aim which the Christian may legitimately set before himself to pursue.

724. BEFRIENDING THE IMMORAL

The circumstances in which it can be right for a Christian to withhold friendship on account of some moral lapse must be very few, for to do that will, in most cases, mean letting someone who most needs moral help be left to the society of people unable to provide it. If we have any responsibility for one another's spiritual welfare we cannot, as a rule, meet that responsibility by methods of ostracism. There may be some cases where action of that kind will be effective in stimulating conscience for the first time. There will be far more where such action will have the effect of merely making the offending person resolute in his resistance to moral claims. You will merely put his back up.

August Twenty-ninth

725. TEACHING OF ST. JOHN BAPTIST

Part of the significance of St. John the Baptist would seem to be this: that he adopted the apocalyptic tone, and that he combined with it all the strong ethical teaching of the prophets: "Repent, for the Kingdom of Heaven is at hand"; the message of the old prophets, "Make yourselves fit," and the message of the apocalyptist, "God is about to act," are by him put together.

726. APOCALYPTIC IMAGERY

Every original genius is hampered by the terms which contemporary language offers as the necessary and sole medium of his self-expression. He must take the best terms available, and trust that his special use of them will gradually correct the suggestions attaching to them, which are alien from his thought, until at last he has imposed his own meaning on them. So the Lord used the language of apocalyptic for certain of His purposes.

727. INNOCENT SUFFERING

The world, starting from a crude notion of justice as consisting in a correlation of pain and guilt, as though so much pain could be regarded as wiping out so much guilt, is bewildered by the suffering of the innocent. The Christian has no interest in solving the problem as thus stated; he must begin by formulating it afresh. For the evil of sin is so great that no amount of pain could ever be regarded as a counterweight. . . . Sin is the setting by man of his will against God's; consciously (when guilt is also involved) or unconsciously. This is the essential evil; no pain is comparable to it.

August Thirtieth

728. INTIMACY WITH GOD

Intimacy with God means becoming filled with love towards everyone—love which means the desire to do what will be good for them and not what will be good or pleasant for us. You see how far that carries us up on the moral struggle against all the disreputable sins.

729. SACRIFICE AND LOVE

Sacrifice need not be painful; its principle is the doing or suffering for love's sake what (apart from love) one would not choose to do or suffer.

730. ALMIGHTY LOVE

Over and over again we are filled with despair because our love is so cold and feeble. No; it is not feeble; it is almighty; for it is God the Holy Ghost, waiting until we give Him opportunity.

August Thirty-first

731. DISHONESTY

It used to be said that an Englishman's word is his bond; and we took it as a clear sign of the corruption of the Italian people when goods could not safely be left in public places such as railway trains—but what we despised in our neighbours is now to be observed among ourselves.

732. "AS GOOD AS GOD"

That is the definition of sin—to fall short of the glory of God! It is not enough that we should be as good as the people about us; nothing is enough except that we should be as good as God— "Ye therefore shall be perfect as your heavenly Father is perfect."

733. THE MEASURE OF SIN

A high ideal may be presented to a man and he considers whether or not he shall accept it for the guidance of his life. His answer must depend on his character. He may give the truest and wisest answer of which he is then capable; but if he has allowed himself to settle down to a selfish outlook or to materialist standards, this will affect his judgment. He will reject the ideal in perfect sincerity; but that sincerity is not so much a justification of his conduct as a measure of his sin.

SEPTEMBER

September First

734. RELIGIOUS FARMER
The farmer who cares for his land and neglects his prayers is, as a farmer, co-operating with God; and the farmer who says his prayers but neglects his land is failing, as a farmer, to co-operate with God. It is a great mistake to suppose that God is only, or even chiefly, concerned with religion.

735. RELIGIOSITY
To talk about receiving a Spirit or even Life is ineffective as a challenge. It easily coheres with a vague religiosity which has no definite and critical moments, no fixed religious practice, no cutting edge.

736. REAL RELIGION
We all know the people who seek to absorb the Spirit of the Creator by contemplation of the beauties of creation—an admirable exercise in itself—instead of anything that could by any stretch of language be called eating the flesh and drinking the blood of the Son of Man.

September Second

737. LIPS AND LIVES
All Christian thanksgiving must take the form of dedication— that we may show forth God's praise not only with our lips but in our lives.

738. RECOGNISING A FACT
Our task is not laboriously to follow Him, nor in some way to transform our nature; our task is to recognise what is already and always fact, that all progress we make is through Him, all knowledge we gain is of Him, all energy we exercise is from Him. *He is the way and the truth and the Life.*

739. LOVE

There is no conceivable combination of circumstances in which it is not possible to show love.

September Third

740. LIMERICK

A limerick which I specially admire illustrates the use of complicated rhythm:

> There once was a gourmet of Crediton
> Who ate *pâté de foie gras*; he spread it on
> A chocolate biscuit
> And said, "I'll just risk it."
> His tomb gives the date that he said it on.

The main merit here is dexterity, dexterity practically divorced from meaning. . . . It is directed to the fulfilment of no particular purpose, but merely achieves its own object with perfect neatness, and so gives us the satisfaction that neatness is able to afford—a limited but quite real satisfaction.

741. LIFE REDEEMED BY BEAUTY

When a man has once faced the terror of life in *Macbeth*, or its horror in *Othello*, or its vast grey gloom in *Hamlet*, or its black darkness shot through with flames of anguish in *King Lear*, and has seen all this not as something repellent but redeemed by beauty and so made sublime, he must be able to face the terrible aspect of life with new courage that is largely born of that experience.

742. IDEALS OF NOVELS

To me it seems that the novels of Dostoievski derive almost the whole of their power and value from the fact that they are interpretations of life in its heights and its depths. . . . I do indeed regard them as among the greatest masterpieces with which I am acquainted, and I think that they show an interpretation of the real meaning both of human life and of the Christian religion in its dealing with human life, of which I know no equal in fiction or other literature.

September Fourth

743. GIFT OF THE CHURCH

Our Christianity is given to us almost, if not quite, entirely by our Christian environment which we call the Church.

744. THE NEW COMMANDMENT

Within the Christian fellowship each is to be linked to each by a love like that of Christ for each. That is the new commandment; and obedience to it is to be the evidence to the world of true discipleship. If the Church really were like that, if every communicant had for every other a love like that of Christ for him, the power of its witness would be irresistible.

745. CHRIST: THE WHOLE VINE

It does not express the whole relation of the Lord to His disciples to say that He is the stem and they the branches, or that He is the Head and they the limbs. He is the whole Vine, the whole Body, and we, as branches or limbs, are "very members incorporate" in Him.

September Fifth

746. ARTIST'S SELF-EXPRESSION

"Art for art's sake" means that an artist's business is to express himself without regard to the question whether he has a self worthy or even fit to be expressed.

747. TRANSFORMATION OF UGLINESS

The climax of art is found when the great artist takes the repellent and hostile elements in experience and, welding them into the completeness of his harmony, makes them—while still in their isolation horrifying—constituent and contributory elements of the sublime.

748. ART IS CONTEMPLATIVE

Art has its life in mental repose—not inactivity, but the activity of still contemplation. The frame round the picture, the curtain at the play's end, are symptomatic. The work of art is a world by itself, to be apprehended by a constant attention, wherein the mind becomes one with the thing it contemplates.

September Sixth

749. FORGIVENESS AND REPENTANCE

We have heard it said over and over again that the promise of the Gospel is that we shall be forgiven if we repent. I should like to point out in passing that our Lord never said that.

750. SELF-EXAMINATION: ACTS AND MOTIVES

There are many aids to self-examination. Some of them are excellent, but some are quite dreadfully bad. I want to suggest how you may know which are the bad ones. If they confront you with a series of questions, all referring to actions, they are bad, because our self-examination must not mainly refer to actions. . . . Let your self-examination, as far as possible, concern motives. Confront yourself with the Christian character as it is set out in the Beatitudes or in St. Paul's articulation of the Fruit of the Spirit or with some other analysis of the mind of Christ. See how far your character corresponds with this, as exhibited in your actions, feelings, plans and hopes.

751. UNSELFISHNESS

The height of unselfishness is to *like* giving up your own pleasures for other people's welfare, because then desire itself is sanctified.

September Seventh

752. ANSWERS TO PRAYER

As we pray for increase of strength or virtue, let us remember that the answer is likely to take the form of opportunity to exercise it, like the lady who prayed for patience and was provided with an ill-tempered cook.

753. FALSE MYSTICISM

The alluring peril of mysticism, according to which a man may have direct experience of unmediated communion with the infinite and eternal God. That is not so; and any experience taken to be this is wrongly interpreted. Only the Son has that direct communion with the Father.

754. PRAYER FOR ENEMIES

Many people are puzzled by the quite clear teaching of Christ that we should pray for our enemies. As far as I can judge from what they say about this, the whole difficulty arises from the supposition that if we pray for anyone we must ask God to give him what he wishes to receive.

September Eighth

755. ULTIMATE UNITY
The unity of all things which philosophers rightly seek is not something which already exists, waiting to be discovered by us, it is something which is being fashioned by toil and strife, by agony and bloody sweat.

756. FREEDOM AND PERSONAL LIKING
No doubt it is true that there are very many people who actually value freedom without associating it in any way with faith in God; but their value for it is merely a personal liking; they have no real answer to the case stated by the philosophers of totalitarianism except that they prefer something else, and in the immense pressures of the modern world that preference will be a feeble bulwark for our threatened liberties.

757. GAMES
The object of a game is the game: there is nothing beyond it. When you begin looking for something beyond it, then you are ruining it. The reason why I gave up golf was that I began to wonder why I should care whether the ball went into the hole or not. It generally didn't. Well, once you begin to question, the game is ruined. You have got to take it mystically, or not at all; for it is an end in itself.

September Ninth

758. CONCEPTUAL THINKING
Conceptual thinking is in its own nature of an interim character, enabling us to enter more fully into the fruition of living experience.

759. INSTRUMENT OF ACTUALISATION
Everyone who utters a significant sentence is actually employing efficient causation as a subordinate instrumentality for the

actualisation of a meaning which determines the sounds or signs that express it and yet may only become actual in those signs and sounds.

760. IMPORTANCE OF MATTER

To deny the real existence of matter is as fatal to a truly spiritual conception of spirit as is materialism, or the denial of all spiritual actuality. For as it is true that matter is the necessary condition for the actuality of life and this also of spirit, so also is it true that, in our experience at least, spirit arises within and as part of an organism which is also material, and expresses its spirituality, not by ignoring matter but by controlling it.

September Tenth

761. MORAL CRITICISM OF "GOD"

It is possible for a man, at least at a certain stage of development, to hold the very highest moral conceptions without any religious life at all, and this is possible not only logically but psychologically. Indeed psychologically there is no doubt about it, for one of the great agencies in the progress of religion has been man's moral criticism of God; that is, of course, of God as understood by him as the time.

762. CONSCIENCE AND RELIGION

The great problem of the religious life arises precisely from the fact that our consciences claim the right, and exercise the right, of criticising God as we know Him. It becomes, therefore, more and more clear that conscience itself is not simply the channel through which belief about God issues into conduct; it is something independent of our religious life.

763. MUTUAL CONFIDENCE

I wonder how many of you could mention on demand the reason which St. Paul gives for telling the truth? It is that "we are members one of another." For that belonging to one another can only exist when there is mutual confidence: the supreme evil of any lie and of any act of dishonesty is that it does something to weaken that mutual confidence.

September Eleventh

764. MONEY

Money exists to facilitate the exchange of goods; it must not be so controlled as to increase the gains of those who hold it at the cost of diminishing the exchange of goods.

765. RIGHT TO PROPERTY

What justifies property and the safeguarding of its rights is that it makes personality fuller, it enables a man to live a fuller life, expressing himself in a greater variety of ways, and therefore it is good for persons to have property. But if so, then it must be good for all persons to have property; and therefore a law of property which results in a few persons having property and the others hardly any cannot be a good law of property.

766. RURAL LANDLORD

The rural landlord discharges many social functions, and ownership of agricultural land, subject to consideration of the public welfare, should not be subject to the same restrictions as ownership of industrial stocks and shares.

September Twelfth

767. A TWOFOLD ACTIVITY

We are brought to Christ and received by Him into the fellowship of His Church; in that company we find the Spirit at work; as we are shaped and moulded by His influence thus diffused and exercised, we begin to find it within ourselves; this individual experience of the Spirit is normally subsequent to, and consequent upon, our experience of His activity in the Church or Christian fellowship. The two stages are marked ritually by Baptism and Confirmation.

768. DORMANT SIN

The teaching of the Lord has the same effect as the Law, which also was from God; it revealed to the dormant conscience the sin that was already there, and it provoked the unconverted will to vigorous obstinacy in its sin.

769. LOVING THE GOOD

There was never a more utterly gross delusion than that "We needs must love the highest when we see it," unless by "see it" we understand "see it for what it is."

September Thirteenth

770. FELLOWSHIP IN VISIBLE ORGANISATION

If fellowship is to be maintained between people whose personal apprehensions of the Gospel are deeply contrasted, it can only be by those bonds of union which a visible organisation alone can secure.

771. ENVIRONMENT

We have our whole being in fellowship with each other, and are what we are because of the tradition that we inherit and the influences that play upon us. Something of our own we bring to this, but only the omniscience of God can discriminate between this original contribution and the work of social influences.

772. ATTITUDE TO ENEMIES

In every form of rivalry or of potential or actual hostility, the Christian citizen should be conscious of his unity in Christ with his fellow Christians on the other side. Often this might turn hostility into co-operation; always it would secure that the hostility, if such there must be, is of action only, never of the heart, and will so prepare the way for reconciliation and restored fellowship.

September Fourteenth

773. ULTIMATE TRUTH

Truth is the perfect correlation of mind and reality; and this is actualised in the Lord's Person. If the Gospel is true and God is, as the Bible declares, a Living God, the ultimate truth is not a system of propositions grasped by a perfect intelligence, but is a Personal Being apprehended in the only way in which persons are ever fully apprehended, that is, by love.

774. RESPONSE TO GLORY OF GOD

Wherever there is response in the hearts of men to the manifested glory of God, whether that manifestation be in nature or in history, there the Spirit of Truth is at work. He inspires all science and all art, and speaks in the conscience of the heathen child.

775. FOUNDING OF KINGDOM OF GOD
The Life Divine is revealed to us as the life of service, which wins men's hearts to itself by absolute self-forgetfulness, and to enter Heaven means to share that life. For the Kingdom of God was founded when its King was crowned with thorns.

September Fifteenth

776. SIN AND SINS
A great many people . . . scarcely know what we mean by the word sin, supposing sin to consist in consciously doing what is known or believed to be wrong. But this is only one part of the whole great fact of sin—the visible part, so to speak. It is the symptom, not the disease; the inflammation, not the poison. All is sin that falls short of God's will for it.

777. ORIGIN OF SELF-REGARD
In principle, the mind could, from the outset, devote itself and its great capacity for free ideas to the yet greater perfection of adjustment within the system of interrelations which it finds. But its range at first is very narrow. It is to be expected that it should start, not with the system as a whole, but with the organism in which it is found, and serve the comfort and convenience of that organism. . . . Thus the whole process of consciously guided action begins in self-centredness.

778. THE DEVIL
Shelve the responsibility for human evil on to Satan if you will; personally I believe he exists and that a large share of that responsibility belongs to him and to subordinate evil spirits. But still you have not escaped the ultimate attribution of evil to the purpose of God. . . . We have still to ask, Why is the devil wicked?

September Sixteenth

779. ULTIMATE UNITY OF CHURCH AND WORLD

The Church's task is to win the world to acceptance of the Gospel till Church and world are one—one altogether not by conversion of the Church into an earthly State but by incorporation of mankind into Christ.

780. CHURCH BEGINNINGS

Men do not constitute the Church by joining it. It was constituted at first by God in calling Abraham from his home upon his journey to the unknown; it was reconstituted by God in Christ, who was at the critical moment the whole Church or People of God.

781. UNION OF ECCLESIASTICAL EXTREMES

It is sad to reflect that when the extreme wings of ecclesiastical opinion are found united, it is usually in resistance to some movement which is afterwards seen to be blessed by God.

September Seventeenth

782. EUCHARIST: RECEPTION

He took the bread, called it His body and broke it; He took the wine, called it His blood and gave it. We do what He did that we may be united to Him in His self-giving, and may receive through His broken Body the power to give ourselves unto death, and through His blood—His life sacrificially offered—may receive the life which is not destroyed by death but rather released by it that it may be united to God for ever.

783. REALITY IS SIGNIFICANCE

The actual significance of any object is more properly called its reality or substance than is its purely physical nature.

784. NON-COMMUNICATING ATTENDANCE AT EUCHARIST

In the case of the Eucharist it is dangerous to form a habit of attending the offering of the Eucharistic sacrifice without receiving the communion of the Body and Blood of Christ whereby we are enabled to be partakers in that sacrifice.

September Eighteenth

785. "LEAD US NOT ..."

No moral adventures, for there is plenty on the straight path of duty to test character and develop grit without our being "led" to the lairs of dragons—"lead us not into temptation."

786. A CONSULTATION

Most of our prayers would be the better if they were completely free from any element of clamour or demand, and had more of the quality of a consultation in which we lay the needs of ourselves and of others before our Father that He may supply them as His loving wisdom suggests.

787. A PRAYER

O God our Judge and Saviour, set before us the vision of thy purity and let us see our sins in the light of thy countenance; pierce our self-contentment with the shafts of thy burning love and let that love consume in us all that hinders us from perfect service of thy cause; for as thy Holiness is our judgment, so are thy wounds our salvation.

September Nineteenth

788. MOB-VIOLENCE AND TYRANTS

Insecurity due to outbreaks of mob-violence is if anything more incompatible with effective freedom of personal living than tyrannous rule by a government of which the principles, and consequently its occasions of tyrannous action, are at least known.

789. "AFTER THE WAR"

While then the terms of this preliminary settlement or truce should contain elements designed to express and bring home to Germany the moral condemnation which she has earned, yet this penal quality should belong only to the truce and not to the permanent settlement. When we reach that stage all thought of corrective justice must be eliminated.

790. REUNION AND CIVIC ACTIVITIES

One reason for pressing forward the work of Christian reunion is that there are essential functions of the Church for which a divided Church is disqualified. But more is needed than reunion in Faith and Order. Roman Catholics have fought each other in national wars despite their unity in Church-membership. What is needed is that the citizen should be conscious of his Churchmanship in his civic activities.

September Twentieth

791. KINGDOM OF GOD SCATTERED

We must ask what was the Word which this Sower had been scattering; it was not exhortation to virtue; it was the proclamation of the Kingdom of God. And it was very hard for men trained in the Jewish tradition to believe that the Kingdom of God is something scattered broadcast, which here meets with failure, there with brief success which gives place to failure, and only occasionally reaches full success.

792. GOD'S PURPOSE

The purpose of God is quite plainly something that can be described in the formula, "The development of persons in community." It is something with two sides to it, and the purpose will be frustrated if either of these receives exclusive attention.

793. THE TRINITY

If a man should repudiate the doctrine of the Trinity simply on the ground that it clashes with his own mathematical conceptions . . . he is like a blind man who should deny the possibility of perspective on the ground that pictures are painted in two dimensions.

September Twenty-first

794. INCARNATION

In Christ's Humanity there is a revelation of Deity such as our sin prevents from being given through ours.

795. SHINING GLORY

The principle that governs the universe "became flesh and dwelt among us and we beheld His glory," and the impression was as of something that shone through Him from beyond—"glory as of an Only Begotten Son from a Father"; of One who perfectly represented something and who is perfectly united with it.

796. THE CROSS AND ITS APPEAL
In perfect obedience to the Will of God and quite alone the Lord went forth bearing His own Cross. In that moment He was in His own person the whole People of God, the true Israel. But by His bearing of the Cross, by the love and obedience both manifested and perfected in total sacrifice, He put forth a power drawing all men to Himself.

September Twenty-second

797. THE TEMPTATIONS
The story of the Temptations is, of course, a parable of His spiritual wrestlings, told by Himself to His disciples. It represents the rejection, under three typical forms, of all existing conceptions of the Messianic task, which was to inaugurate the Kingdom of God.

798. CHRIST'S CLAIMS
If He is a very good man completely surrendered to the Spirit of God, He cannot, without offence, speak as the Johannine Christ speaks. But if He is God come in the flesh He not only may, He must proclaim Himself as the fount of salvation.

799. CHRIST AND THE GOSPELS
The Gospels were written by members of the Church for their fellow members, and each is "The Gospel according to" somebody. What reaches us is never a certified record but always a personal impression. Thus our concern is always with the Christ of faith, not with some supposed different Jesus of history.

September Twenty-third

800. SIN AND CRIME
Not every sinful action is a crime, nor is it desirable to make it so; but in a well-ordered State every crime is also a sin.

801. DIGNITY OF MAN v. STATE
First and foremost are the two great principles of the divine Fatherhood and Man's eternal destiny, because these two assure

to the individual a status and a dignity which are prior to his membership of any earthly state, so that the State must always treat him as someone who has a value other than his value to itself.

802. CHURCH AND STATE IN SWEDEN
In Sweden the King prescribes the texts on which sermons shall be preached on many Sundays in the year; but the submission is not all on one side, for the Synod has the right to veto an Act of Parliament dealing with a moral issue, and has exercised that right within the last twelve years.

September Twenty-fourth

803. UTOPIANISM
Let us remember that when we pass from the realm of pure principle to the realm of action it is our duty as Christians to think out that kind of action which is practicable in the world we know with such human nature as ours, and that of our neighbours as its agent; not to dream of what would be a perfect world if everyone already were a perfect Christian.

804. AID OF LAW
You and I still need the law in our private lives to strengthen us in our weaker moments. It was a Master of Balliol who said: "Personally, I *prefer* to purchase my railway ticket, but doubtless the presence of a ticket inspector has often clinched the matter!" The law which upholds our purpose to lead an honest life is not a limitation of our freedom, but rather the support and stay of it.

805. TWO DUTIES
There are two duties, each relatively easy to fulfil in isolation, not easy to combine; they may be expressed in two apostolic injunctions which themselves are offered in combination: "Quench not the spirit; hold fast that which is good."

September Twenty-fifth

806. INTERNATIONAL FINANCE

The profit motive in industry and in finance, when given such freedom and prominence as it now has, becomes a profoundly and pervasively disturbing factor. The one thing that has become international in our world is finance; it is arguable that it ought to have been the last.

807. COMMONWEALTH

We may cut the knot by following Sir Richard Acland in his demand for universal communal ownership. I shrink from this, because I think that the administration of the communal property would tend to become bureaucratic and mechanical.

808. BOLSHEVISM AND CLASSES

The Communists won power in Russia by violence, and have taken the first steps towards a classless society by "liquidating" the other classes; the result, if it were possible that they should succeed, would not be a truly classless society, but a one-class society.

September Twenty-sixth

809. DESIRE CONVERTED

The coming of the Holy Spirit in power is due to the action of the Son in revealing the love of the Father, and . . . one way of summarising the purpose of Christ's coming is to say that He came in order that the Spirit might come. That inward power of God converting desire itself is a result of the disclosure of the love of God and the response which it wins.

810. JUDGMENT

He draws us by His love; and men are never so free as when they act from the love in their hearts which love shown to them has called forth. If, then, I come by my own will yet because the Father draws me, so also it is the Father who is taking me away if I depart by my own will. He offers me the love divine; it draws me or repels me, according to the condition of my will. It had repelled Judas. . . . His going was an act of defiance on his part;

it was an act of condemnation and execution on the part of God. This is the thought of judgment everywhere presented in this Gospel.

811. TRADITIONAL INFLUENCE
Even apart from religion, the inner quality in which we place our trust is the deposit of the tradition in which we were brought up, of the influence of parents and teachers. We could not civilise ourselves. If we had been carried off in infancy to live among savages, we should be savages now.

September Twenty-seventh

812. FELLOWSHIP OF DIVERSE CONVICTIONS
Our own convictions may possibly not exhaust the whole range of truth. . . . and the cause of truth is best served by the maintenance of fellowship in one body of those whose convictions are even widely divergent.

813. COMMUNITY
Men work in herds at their appointed tasks of mass-production; certainly that is the reverse of solitude, but a mass or crowd is not a community, because in it the individuality of each man is irrelevant.

814. PERSONAL FELLOWSHIP WITH CHRIST
The fellowship of the Christian with his Lord does not in the smallest degree resemble the kind of communication which spiritualists believe to be possible between the spirits of the departed and ourselves. It is an intimate, personal fellowship. Of course, it is possible to regard it as an hallucination; but it is a remarkably persistent one. It arises under the most astonishing conditions, and above all it happens to men of every race and of every period.

September Twenty-eighth

815. COLLEGIATE RESPONSIBILITIES
May I suggest that the resident Fellow of a College who, being a professed Christian, is not frequent and regular in attendance at the daily service in his College chapel, is a fraudulent trustee for the treasure committed to him in his own faith?

816. CHRISTIANS IN A UNIVERSITY

The member of a College, senior or junior, must not think of himself . . . as first and foremost a member of that College who happens, privately and incidentally, to be a Christian, but must think of himself, and by his conversation and conduct lead others to think of him, as first and foremost a Christian whose sphere of active discipleship is the College of which he is a member.

817. RELIGIOUS NEUTRALITY

To be neutral concerning God is the same thing as to ignore and deny Him. This is one of those questions to which the answer "No" is automatically given unless you deliberately give the answer "Yes"; to give no answer is to answer, "No."

September Twenty-ninth

818. SEEING ANGELS

When men "see" or "hear" angels, it is rather to be supposed that an intense interior awareness of a divine message leads to the projection of an image which is then experienced as an occasion of something seen and heard. That divine messengers were sent and divine messages received we need not doubt; that they took physical form so that all who "saw" anything must "see" the same thing we need not suppose.

819. CONSEQUENCE OF GLORY

The Cross is the glory of God because self-sacrifice is the expression of love. That glory would be complete in itself even if it had no consequences. But in fact what is revealed in the Cross is not only the perfection of the divine love, but its triumph. For by its sacrifice the divine love wins those who can appreciate it out of their selfishness which is spiritual death into loving fellowship with itself which is true life.

820. GOD'S JUDGMENTS

Those consequences which follow from our actions or characters by the operation of God's laws are His judgments upon us.

September Thirtieth

821. JUSTICE, EXPRESSION OF LOVE

Justice is the first expression of love. It is not something contrary to love, which love mitigates and softens. It is the first expression of it that must be satisfied, before the other and higher expressions can rightly find their places.

822. CONDONING EVIL

Justice is inevitably stern. It refuses merely to overlook wrongs that have been done. God, in Christ, does not overlook wrongs that have been done, but takes them into Himself. And perhaps, if you thought we really had the spiritual power to take these evils unto ourselves, and so negate them by meeting them with perfect love, that might be the right way to treat them. But we cannot do it. If we dream of that we deceive ourselves, and the result, in fact, will be something very different; it will be a condoning of the evil, and that is worse than all.

823. VOCATION AND PENSION

Adventure and loyalty to Christ is what we want. We want it in men's choice of a career. Nothing depresses me so much as a young man who, when thinking what career he shall take up, begins discussing the prospects of a pension.

OCTOBER

October First

824. A PRIOR DUTY

It is not enough that a man should always do what he thinks to be his duty; there is an even prior duty to that, namely that, he should think to be his duty what really is his duty. All the deepest sins in the nature of most of us are sins that we have not discovered at all. They are very often associated with something about us with which we are particularly well satisfied. . . . And that means we cannot rely implicitly upon our consciences.

825. OBEDIENCE AND REVELATION

Every revelation of God is a demand, and the way to knowledge of God is by obedience.

826. SLUMS

By miracles of grace, even in the worst housing conditions some beautiful lives are led; but we know quite well that most slum-dwellers very largely succumb to their conditions morally. It is especially hard for the children who grow up in those conditions; to know that there are stumbling-blocks in the way of Christ's little ones and to leave them there is not very different from putting them there; and we know what He had to say about that.

October Second

827. VICTORY OF THE CROSS

The Cross is not for Christians a stumbling-block which the Resurrection has removed; it is not a defeat of which the effect has been cancelled by a subsequent victory. It is itself the triumph. What was the devil's worst is become God's best.

828. THE GOSPEL

It is not the mere occurrence of its several episodes that constitutes the Gospel; it is their spiritual and eternal significance; but part of their spiritual and eternal significance is their physical and temporal occurrence.

829. LIBERAL PROTESTANTISM
Why anyone should have troubled to crucify the Christ of Liberal Protestantism has always been a mystery.

October Third
830. SECTS
Remote from the true conception of the Ministry would be the action of a group of persons who should select one of their own number to say to them the things which they desired to hear.

831. DENOMINATIONAL DIVISIONS
It is part of the evil of our religious divisions that the State cannot merely endow religious activities, exercising only such vigilance as would ensure that its bounty is not abused. If all citizens were members of one Church it could do this, if the citizens being also Churchmen approved; and this might well be an ideal arrangement. Thus all schools might be in practice controlled by the Church and financed by the State. Our divisions make this impossible.

832. CHURCH ENDOWMENT
The Church, as Church, has no interest in establishment, endowment, or any such thing. Its officers and members are very much interested in these matters as Christian citizens or even as personally affected, but not as members of the Body of Christ who had not where to lay His head.

October Fourth
833. CONTROL OF MATTER
Christianity conceives the spiritual as a power controlling the material and becoming actual in that control, so that in its understanding of the world matter exists to be the vehicle of spirit, and spirit is actual in its exercise of control over matter.

834. MATERIAL AND SPIRITUAL
We so commonly contrast "material" and "spiritual" that we easily suppose matter and spirit to be mutually exclusive opposites. For Christians this is certainly not true; indeed Christianity is the most materialist of all the great religions.

835. CHRISTIAN DIVISIONS

The greatest divisions of Christendom are geographical. . . . The first great division was that of East and West, which was between a mentality dominated by metaphysic and a mentality dominated by law. The next was within the West between North and South, between a traditional love of local autonomy and a traditional love of centralised unity.

October Fifth

836. TIME PROCESS AND MORAL EFFECTIVENESS

It is sheer lack of imagination to suppose that a vista of a million million years can give more significance than a week or a fortnight to our moral strivings, if at the end it is all to be as though we have never been at all.

837. WAR AND THE CHRISTIAN

The primary question for a Christian is not: Are there any circumstances in which it is right that my country should go to war? but: Are we to acquiesce in regarding war as the only way, or as a tolerable way, of settling international disputes when they arise? And the Christian is bound by every principle of the Gospel to answer, No.

838. CORPORATE LOYALTY

The Christian citizen who is a member or officer of any association must work loyally with the association. He is not at liberty to think out for himself what is on Christian grounds the best course of action and then take that course. He may commend it to his fellow members; and if he persuades them he and they will follow it together. But he is bound to act with the association or withdraw from it.

October Sixth

839. MY BROTHER'S KEEPER?

If there is anybody who professes not to believe that other people can have any claim upon him, or that he is in any way concerned with their welfare, I know of no way of answering him by argument. The only method with which I am acquainted is to trap him into admitting what he has just denied, as Socrates trapped Callicles in the Gorgias.

840. ECONOMICS A.D. 30?

It seems possible at first to argue that all moral conceptions are simply derived from economic forces, and that by reorganising the economic forces and those akin to them we shall reorganise people's moral conceptions and regenerate them. . . . But I would simply ask one question, and there leave the matter. What is there peculiar about the economic, social or political organisation of Palestine in the first centuries B.C. and A.D., which accounts for the life of Christ?

841. CREED AND THE MORAL SENSE

Religion must commend itself to the moral sense, and, therefore, we cannot claim that the moral sense is dependent upon our creed.

October Seventh

842. MY ABSOLUTE DUTY

It is my absolute duty to will the right; but there is no act which it is my absolute duty, independently of circumstances, to do or not to do. Murder is always wrong, because murder is such killing as is wrong; but it is often open to dispute whether or not a particular instance of killing is murder.

843. DUTY TO GOD

It is our duty to God to give our whole attention to the task He has appointed for us—whether that be preaching the Gospel or ploughing the field. In either case we must not be wrapped in communion with God while we do it.

844. THE WORLD AND THE SPIRITUAL LIFE

For a long way in the spiritual life you have got the world helping you. It is going to help you against the grosser temptations of the flesh, for example. The world is going to help you in your fight against the sins of hatred and malice, because the world likes a kindly and genial nature. But when you come to your struggle with the world, the world is going to be on the wrong side, as when you find that what Christ requires is something which people about you will consider quite foolish and fantastic.

October Eighth

845. SELF-COMPLACENCY

We are distressed about some special fault, and ask His aid to overcome it; whereupon He tells us that our real trouble is our self-complacence and self-reliance, and if it is His help that we seek, He will rouse us from these. But we do not want that at all. Indeed our chief reason for wanting to overcome that special fault was that it disturbed our self-complacence, which we hoped, after a little moral effort, to enjoy once more.

846. PACIFISM

A thoroughly Christian nation, I believe, would refuse to fight even in self-defence if only its own interest were at stake; but I do not think it follows at all that the Christian citizen of a state which has not yet reached that pitch should refuse to fight, because if he does he may be putting himself entirely out of touch with the great stream of life which at the moment may be a far nobler thing than any practicable alternative.

847. CITIZENS AND WAR

In the case of war, we must distinguish the temper of mind which encourages war, and the consent to fight for one's country when once war is declared. Those are quite different points.

October Ninth

848. DESCARTES

If I were asked what was the most disastrous moment in the history of Europe I should be strongly tempted to answer that it was that period of leisure when René Descartes, having no claims to meet, remained for a whole day "shut up alone in a stove."

849. MIND AND MATTER

It is hardly conceivable that the revision of Physics will go so far as to assert that the vagaries of electrons are due to appreciation of apparent good on the part of electrons, or in other words to their own choice. Till that assertion is made, the essential difference between mind and matter remains.

850. DETERMINISM NONSENSE
Stark Determinism is stark nonsense, not only in Ethics but in every other field of study; for it declares that all objects are constituted by their external relations; and, if so, the process of mutual determination can never start. . . . Stark Determinism presents us with the spectacle of nothing-at-all differentiating itself into this richly varied universe through the mutual interaction of its non-existent parts.

October Tenth

851. GOD'S FOUR GIFTS
There are four requisites for life which are given by the bounty of God—air, light, land and water. These exist before man's labour is expended upon them, and upon air and light man can do nothing except spoil them.

852. ECONOMIC AIM
If we let the economic aim become predominant, we shall find that it disintegrates our society, that it treats every individual primarily as so much labour power to be used where he most conduces to efficiency of output, irrespective of all his social ties and traditional roots. The economic approach to life atomises society.

853. DARWINISM
. . . The quite unwarrantable interpretation of Darwinism as giving the clue to moral progress: for the survival of the fittest was taken to mean the survival of the best.

October Eleventh

854. REPENTANCE AND FORGIVENESS
"You shall be forgiven if you repent." But how can I repent; I only do wrong things because I like them; I cannot stop liking them because you tell me not to like them any more; I can only stop liking them if I become a new kind of person or I see them in some new perspective. It is no use to tell a man he will be

forgiven if he will repent, unless you can tell him how to repent. As Coleridge truly said, the supreme merit of the Gospel is not that it promises forgiveness to those who repent, but that it promises repentance to those who sin, if only they will truly put their faith into practice.

855. Forgiveness

One man may freely forgive an offending brother without waiting for any previous repentance, and also without giving the impression that he condones the wrong, while another will give that impression and therefore can rightly forgive only when repentance precedes.

856. Self-examination

As a matter of wisdom in the handling of souls, I cannot help thinking we have attended too much to the bad moments which have issued in sinful acts, and have not usually sufficiently urged people to make the most of their best times, because those are the times when there is hope.

October Twelfth

857. Means of Exchange and Manipulation

The principle that money should function as a means of exchange, and that those who have the handling of it should receive no doubt a perfectly reasonable remuneration for their integrity and their honesty in dealing with it, but not have the opportunity, by that mere manipulation, of creating new values for themselves which do not correspond to any useful services offered by them to the community—that is, I think, an undoubtedly sound principle.

858. Social Purpose of Money

Money is in its own nature a medium of exchange, and therefore, if you use it as a commodity in the sense of trying to profit yourself by variations in its value over against goods, you are destroying it for its proper social purpose; and there are some kinds of activity in that direction which I think public opinion is tending to think ought undoubtedly to be prohibited, as for example, speculation in foreign currencies. This is not a crime of the banks, which never, I believe, indulge in this evil practice. It is a crime of the private fortune-hunter.

859. Just Price

The doctrine of the just price was that you are entitled to charge, for what you sell, what covers the cost to you plus a reasonable return as estimated by the current habit of society, and the kind of position that society was expecting you to maintain. In those days, society had a fairly rigid structure—it was not so fluid as we are now, it was a society more of status than of contract as the phrase used to be.

October Thirteenth

860. Democracy

Where people are ready to work democratic institutions, they more fully conform to the principle of the sanctity of personality than any other type.

861. Divorce of Church and State

The growing distinction between Church and State may make it more difficult for the Church to permeate the State and direct it from within; it makes it easier for the Church, as a consciously distinct body, to impinge upon the State and influence it from without.

862. Law as Aid to Good Life

Very few citizens are so established in virtue as to be able to dispense with the support of the law and its penalties without moral deterioration.

October Fourteenth

863. "Deserving Poor"

Our Lord made no inquiries of the people who came to Him for a boon as to whether they were deserving or not.

864. "Let Him Suffer"

No Christian will ever dream of saying, "It is his own fault; now let him suffer for it." If Christ had taken that line, where would our redemption be?

865. Strengthening Motive

The fear of punishment is a motive either entirely selfish or almost entirely selfish. That is the chief reason why punishment, which cannot be altogether abolished without disaster to other members of a community than the actual culprit, should always be kept at a minimum, for a motive is strengthened when appeals are made to it.

October Fifteenth

866. SCIENCE

Science has its life in mental restlessness; it asks of every fact the questions Why? or How? and of the answer it asks Why? or How? again.

867. UNIFORM CAUSAL PROCESSES

If the older scientific view of uniform causal processes ultimately prevails, for this the theist has his explanation, both in the constancy of the Divine Nature which will vary its activity only for sufficient reason, and in the need for substantial uniformity as a basis for moral action.

868. SCIENTIFIC IGNORANCE

Science does not in the least know why evolution goes forward at all; it can only trace out some of the laws in accordance with which it moves forward. . . . If the initiation of a new species always is some spontaneous variation, what is the word "spontaneous" except a confession of ignorance? What caused it to happen?

October Sixteenth

869. GROWTH OF CHURCH

The Church is growing now, and for the last forty years has been growing, faster than at any previous period in its history. And where it grows it creates fellowship.

870. THE HOLY CHURCH

The primary characteristic of the Church is neither its missionary enterprise which is the essence of Apostolicity, nor its universal scope which is its Catholicity, but the fact that it is constituted by the redeeming act of God in Christ and is sustained by the indwelling divine Spirit, or in short its Holiness. And the first way in which it is called to be itself is neither through missionary extension nor through influence upon national life but through inward sanctification.

871. CLOUDED LIGHT IN CHURCH
In the Church the true light shines because in it the Gospel is read and the Bread of Life is offered. If these be not done, there is no Church at all. But the world which looks on may never see the light because the lives of the members of the Church, including those who read that Gospel and offer that Bread, betray the treasure entrusted to them.

October Seventeenth

872. EUCHARIST BREAD AND WINE
To express my own thought accurately I must say, not that the Bread and Wine symbolise, or are symbols of, the Body and Blood of Christ, but that sacramentally (i.e. symbolically and instrumentally) they *are* His Body and Blood; that is to say, within the sacramental action that is their value and therefore their reality.

873. RECEIVING THE COMMUNION
It is not as a detached individual Christian that I receive the Holy Communion. It is as a member of Christ's Body, the Church. What I need—(I do not say "desire," but what I spiritually need)— is to escape from any such narrowly limited fellowship as depends on feelings of the moment, that I may be helped to the realisation, so far more difficult, of fellowship in the whole Communion of Saints.

874. PLEADING CHRIST'S SACRIFICE
Because of the sacrifice of Christ . . . we are able with confidence to "draw near" and offer ourselves a living sacrifice to the Father. We have no right to the confidence if we forget its condition. To remember the condition as we approach the Father is of itself to offer and plead . . . that one sacrifice as our all-sufficient justification.

October Eighteenth

875. "WHO ARE MY FRIENDS?"

"Greater love than this hath no man, that a man lay down his life on behalf of his friends." Some have said: Is it not greater love to die for enemies than for friends? But this overstresses the word *friends*. It does not here represent those who love Him but those whom he loves; the saying declares that love has no more complete expression than death on behalf of those to whom it is directed; the distinction between those who return that love and those who do not, does not arise.

876. HUMILITY AND SERVICE

Man's humility does not begin with the giving of service; it begins with the readiness to receive it. For there can be much pride and condescension in our giving of service. It is wholesome only when it is offered spontaneously on the impulse of real love; the conscientious offer of it is almost sure to "have the nature of sin," as almost all virtue has of which the origin is in our own deliberate wills.

877. INDEPENDENCE

The desire "not to be beholden to anybody" is completely un-Christian.

October Nineteenth

878. NOVEL-READING

I am one of those who, when reading a novel, wish for two things if possible. I wish for events; I want things to happen; and also I want the people to be agreeable company. Now that of course puts me out of court with the enormous bulk of modern literature which steadily refuses to bring forward the character of any person with whom you could endure to spend half an hour in real life.

879. THRILLERS

Although I do not claim for the thriller that it is a very exalted type of literature, I do claim for it that it is already beginning to show quite definite moral qualities.

880. Prose and Poetry

Prose and verse are a contrasted pair of terms dealing with the rhythm in which the words are put together. Poetry and science are contrasted terms dealing with the habit of mind in which the object in question is being regarded.

October Twentieth

881. Profit Motive

There is no harm in the profit motive as such. It is perfectly reasonable that a man should want to give to his children a better chance than he had himself. It has its own right place, but that is not the first place. And it is the predominance of the profit motive—the fact that it comes first in the determination of so much of our economic and industrial activity that is a great evil.

882. Guaranteeing the Public Interest

However high-minded and public-spirited the directors of a privately owned concern may be, they will, five times out of six, be bound to put first the purely economic interests of what they are working rather than the public interest; and if they do put the public interest first, how are we to know that they are qualified to estimate it properly? They are not chosen for the purpose. They will quite rightly say it is not their function. If we want the public interest put first, we must so organise our life that those who are chosen for their concern with and qualification to judge the public interest, are in positions of control.

883. Religion Nothing without Miracles

Demand for miracle is absolutely inherent in religion. Either religion is nothing at all for us, or else it is belief in a power which enables a man to do what without his religion he could not do—that is, to act in ways which the study of natural science will never lead us to understand.

October Twenty-first

884. MISERABLE SINNERS

When we put our lives in that way, side by side with the mind of Christ, are any of us going to say that the language traditionally put into our mouths is exaggerated? Some people say they do not like to call themselves "miserable sinners." If by "miserable" they mean "unhappy," that may be right; they may be perfectly happy sinners. They may be the kind of people who would be happy in hell, because they fitted it. But if by "miserable" they mean deserving of pity, then are any of us going to deny that we are pitiable sinners?

885. BAD HABITS

Lift the stone—the stone which shuts the soul into its tomb of anxiety, or worry, or resentment. It involves the exposure of habits grown horrible in their rigidity. But it is the condition of response to the quickening voice.

886. SATANIC CHARACTER

The reason our Lord gave for calling one of His disciples "Satan" was that he thought like a man instead of thinking like God—for that he was called "Satan."

October Twenty-second

887. PURPOSE OF THE GIFT

This is the primary purpose for which the Spirit is given; that we may bear witness to Christ. We must not expect the gift while we ignore the purpose. A Church which ceases to be missionary will not be, and cannot rightly expect to be, "spiritual."

888. THE CONDITION OF THE GIFT

To the Church as the fellowship of the Spirit is given the authority of Christ Himself as Pardoner and Judge. But only so far as the Church in and through its members fulfils the condition—*Receive holy spirit*—can it discharge this function.

889. HATING CHRISTIANITY

Not all that the world hates is good Christianity; but it does hate good Christianity and always will.

October Twenty-third

890. PERJURY AND ADULTERY

The guilty party is, *eo ipso*, excommunicated for adultery. If, in fact, he did not commit adultery but deliberately provided evidence to convince a court that he did, he is morally guilty of perjury, and at any rate has no ground for complaint if he is treated by the Church as having done what he deliberately persuaded a Court that he did; such conduct in any case can be but little better than adultery itself.

891. CONTRACEPTIVES

The use of contraceptives can only properly be considered if the obligation of parenthood is first fully recognised, and if it is also fully recognised that self-control remains a binding duty.

892. UNMARRIED INTIMACY

It is not the duty of unmarried persons to foster relations of intensely intimate affection for other persons of either sex; on the contrary, it is their duty to avoid and suppress such feelings except in the one instance of a love which looks forward to marriage and its intimacy as its own fulfilment.

October Twenty-fourth

893. KING'S CORONATION

In the English Coronation service the King is seated as the token of earthly royalty is placed upon his head; but he is kneeling when just afterwards he receives the effectual tokens of divine grace in the same manner in which any labourer in any village church receives them. At the point where alone man has true dignity he is completely equal to all his fellow men; his infinite value is of such a kind as to shut out all superiority.

894. BELIEF AND CONDUCT

A false belief is worse than any wrong action, because it leads to innumerable wrong actions. How often we hear the old silly saying that it does not matter what a man believes, and that this is a private affair between a man and his Maker.

895. The Second Commandment

To worship a false god is the worst thing a man can do—far worse than deliberate atheism, worse even than careless neglect of the true God when we know something about Him.

October Twenty-fifth

896. Belief and Action

We all want to *do* things, partly out of a just eagerness that evils should be remedied, partly out of a desire to justify ourselves. . . . The first necessity is to *believe on* Him. This is different from believing things about Him, though that may be one preliminary. It means trusting Him as a man trusts his friend—rather as a child trusts his father.

897. Faith and Belief

Faith is always something very much more than belief; it is practical and personal trust; and when you trust in somebody with completeness the result is that his will begins to direct your own, again freely, because your trust must be freely given or else it is not trust at all. But if his will directs your own, then, in a very real moral sense, you are incorporated into his personality or, as the New Testament would say, into His body.

898. Faith and Personal Experience

With all of us faith in God begins because of our faith in those who tell us of Him. This may be fully real, and have strength to "save" the soul. But it is less than the faith which rests on a personal experience, which has already in some measure supplied to faith its vindication and verification.

October Twenty-sixth

899. Historical Selection

In the presentation of history selection is inevitable. If the historian has no consciously accepted principle of selection, he will be guided by principles or influences to which he pays no attention, so that he cannot in any way check them or control them.

900. PHARISAISM OF THE PUBLICAN

A great preacher in England once said of the English people that their besetting sin was the pharisaism of the Publican; they do not thank God that they are not as other men are; they thank God that they *are* as other men are—which is much worse.

901. PUBLIC OPINION

Public opinion does not consist of what people think; it consists of that part of what people think which they express.

October Twenty-seventh

902. LAW AND MORALS

Legislation is really the fruit of moral advance, and not the cause of it.

903. COMMUNISM NO ANSWER

Communism seeks to create by force a world of mutual co-operation, believing that those who grow up in such a world will be freed from acquisitiveness and self-concern. But the effect will only be to direct these motives upon other objects than wealth, such as honour and influence. And the initial trust in force, which is always an appeal to self-concern, will stimulate the sentiment which it aims at destroying.

904. NATIONAL VOCATION

The God whose Majesty is specially revealed in the act of the Lord washing His disciples' feet, will not call His strong nations to lord it over the rest of His family. There may be need, even a divine call, to stand by force for righteousness against an unrighteous abuse of force; but the notion of an essentially conquering mission is incompatible with the character of God revealed in Christ.

October Twenty-eighth

905. THE WORLD CHURCH

As though in preparation for such a time as this, God has been building up a Christian fellowship which now extends into almost every nation, and binds citizens of them all together in true unity and mutual love. No human agency has planned this.

It is the result of the great missionary enterprise of the last hundred and fifty years.

906. MISSIONARY MOTIVE

Neither the missionaries nor those who sent them out were aiming at the creation of a world-wide fellowship interpenetrating the nations, bridging the gulfs between them, and supplying the promise of a check to their rivalries. The aim for nearly the whole period was to preach the Gospel to as many individuals as could be reached so that those who were won to discipleship should be put in the way of eternal salvation. Almost incidentally the great world-fellowship has arisen; it is the great new fact of our era.

907. AFRICA AND THE EAST

When the East is converted and has given us its power of mystic contemplation, raised to the highest pitch by union with Christ; when Africa is converted, and has given us the treasure of its child-like affection and devotion, raised to its highest pitch by contact with Christ; then there will come back to us from converted India and converted Africa the power which may enable us to complete the work of making England into a province of the Kingdom of God.

October Twenty-ninth

908. MORTGAGES

I am not sure what the theological moralists would have said about systems of mortgaging and the like, but they would have been very shy of them. Perhaps it is the only way in the modern world in which the necessary—quite necessary—security can be obtained; but there is something always rather anxious about it, because, as I have said, behind all these Christian principles there always lay the primary demand that on no account should the stronger exploit the weaker.

909. MAXIMUM OUTPUT

While the economist has his special and indispensable place in telling us what are the probable effects of any proposed activities, that does not of itself give us any direction about what we should do. We still have to choose between the various goals of activity, and ask the economist how we may then best pursue them. But if we leave him to himself, he will inevitably keep maximum output first as the one true end, and it is not.

910. USURY

The discussion: *What does constitute usury?* has bothered the Church perpetually. I wish it were bothering us now, because it is that kind of mental trouble which stimulates the public conscience. You can focus attention upon a principle when there is public debate how it ought to be applied far better than if there is no such debate; and, if we could start discussing what kind of loans ought to be regarded as usurious and therefore immoral, it would, I think, help us a long way forward.

October Thirtieth

911. THE EARLY CHURCH

When we go back to the first records of the Church we find neither a Ministry which called people into association with it, nor an undifferentiated fellowship which delegated powers to a Ministry; but we find a complete Church, with the Apostolate accepted as its focus of administration and authority.

912. LOYALTY AND "OTHER BODIES"

Let us set ourselves to gain a deepening loyalty to our Anglican tradition of Catholic order, Evangelical immediacy in our approach to God, and Liberal acceptance of new truth made known to us; and let us at the same time join with all our fellow Christians who will join with us in bearing witness to the claim of Christ to rule in every department of human life, and to the principles of His Kingdom.

913. INDIAN MORALITY

The Indian may be less ready than the Englishman to tell the truth, but he is more ready to give his goods to feed the poor. Vicarious suffering and the refusal to resist evil are not strange or shocking to him.

October Thirty-first

914. CRUCIFIXION

A sinful world redeemed by such a sacrifice as the Crucifixion of Christ is better than a world that had never sinned.

915. COMING OF SON OF MAN

So when any civilisation falls through repudiation of some one or another of the principles of Christ, whether that repudiation be shown in the maintenance of slavery, or in the denial of personal freedom, or in the clinging to such privilege and inequality as break up the fellowship of society, in every such catastrophe we see the Son of Man come with power.

916. TRANSMUTATION OF VALUE

The event or act which in isolation is evil can be itself an integral and contributing part of a whole which, as a whole, is good. . . . The crucifixion of Christ is supremely bad when taken in isolation, but when taken as part of the whole scheme of which it is the pivot, it is supremely good.

NOVEMBER

November First

917. FUTURE LIFE

As far as I know there is nothing in the world I am so sure of, but I have no sort of picture of it and I don't feel the smallest desire for one. I should know it would be wrong and therefore I think I am happier without one.

918. "HIGHER SERVICE"

I don't much like the modern way of saying "Passed to higher service." There is no difference between one service and another, because the highest service is to do what God wants of you here and now and there is nothing higher than that in the seventh heaven. I like 'the wider life' better. There is every reason to suppose that it is a removal of limitations.

[*Words said to Mrs. Temple while walking round the garden at Bishopthorpe on two different occasions, when they were talking about the future life.—From Mrs. Temple's letter after the death of her husband* (December, 1944).]

919. COMMUNION OF SAINTS

We, if we truly lift up our hearts to the Lord and find that we are not alone with Him, but are in the company of Angels and Archangels and all the whole company of heaven, may find in that Communion of all the Saints which overleaps all divisions and blots out all the bitterness of human strife, a bond of unity which may enable us to do something of great moment towards healing the wounds of the world.

November Second

920. SPIRITUALISM

It is positively undesirable that there should be experimental proof of man's survival of death. It might or might not encourage the belief that God exists; it would certainly, as I think, make very much harder the essential business of faith, which is the transference of the centre of interest and concern from self to God.

921. The Universal Word

There is no man in the world in whom this logos, this Word of God, this rational principle of all things, does not speak. The veriest atheist of them all thinks by the power of that which is perfectly revealed in Jesus Christ. It is the light that lighteth every man. You never get away from it, and there is nobody who is without it. That light which lighteth every man, and which shone by fits and starts elsewhere, that Word which was spoken in divers portions and divers manners in the prophets, shone out supremely and found perfect utterance in the Son.

922. Good Friday

"There cannot be a God of love," men say, "because if there were, and He looked upon this world, His heart would break."

The Church points to the Cross and says, "His heart does break."

"It is God who has made the world," men say, "it is He who is responsible, and it is He who should bear the load."

The Church points to the Cross and says, "He does bear it."

"God is beyond men's comprehension, and it is blasphemy to say you know Him"; and the Church answers, "We do not know Him perfectly; but we worship the majesty we see."

November Third

923. Temptation in the Wilderness

He might bribe men to obey Him by the promise of good things, and so encourage man's evil tendency to care more for creature comforts than for the Word of God. He might coerce men to obey by threat of penalty, as earthly rulers do, and so Himself worship, and encourage men to worship, the Prince of this world. He might offer irresistible proof so that men would have to think the Gospel true even if they wished that it were not, putting to the proof the God who claims men's trust. In other words, all the rejected methods are essentially appeals to self-interest.

924. Character of Jesus

What we find is power in complete subordination to love; and that is something like a definition of the Kingdom of God.

925. The Second Coming

In power the Kingdom was established when Christ was lifted up upon the Cross. From that moment it is true that "He cometh with clouds"; that is present fact. He reigns from the Tree. But not all have eyes to perceive; and the time when "every eye shall see Him" is still future, and this is the truth in the expectation of a Return or Second Coming.

November Fourth

926. Historic Episcopate

I am convinced that the Anglican Communion is right to maintain its insistence on the Historic Episcopate, but I am equally convinced that Anglicans think far too much—not necessarily too highly, but assuredly too often and too long—of that same Episcopate. It would be far better for us if we could take it for granted and give our undistracted thought to other matters.

927. Freedom to Order Worship

There are features of the present "Establishment" in England which seem to me to be in the proper sense intolerable. The Church as a fellowship of worshippers ought to have absolute freedom to order its own worship without any restriction from persons and representatives of persons who may or may not be members of that fellowship.

928. Christians and Problems

Over and over again the Church has no message whatever in regard to the existing situation. It can only say, "If you will but look at it in a quite different way from that in which you are regarding it, there will be no problem and the threat will vanish away. But how you had better adjust the result of your sin while you remain in your sin, is necessarily a question with which the Church has nothing to do."

November Fifth

929. An Emaciated Synthesis

When people suggest that what we need is the gathering together of the best elements in all religions and the making of a new one out of them, it may be worth while to inquire first whether

Christianity has not already done it. Supposing such a religion was formed, gathering together what most people regard as the best elements of the various faiths now in the world, it would itself become a distinctive religion, and someone would come afterwards and urge the very same course in regard to all religions then existing, including our new emaciated synthesis; so it would go on for ever.

930. DISTINCTIVE MOMENTS IN RELIGIONS
We cannot remind ourselves too often that the things which make religion valuable are the things which distinguish religions from each other.

931. THE GULF BRIDGED
The gulf between man and God is bridged, not by man's achievement, but by God's humiliation.

November Sixth

932. BEGINNING PRAYER
You should never begin to pray until you have the figure of Christ before your mind, and should pray to God as you see Him there.

933. WHY PRAY?
We pray because the realisation that God is the source of all good may be the condition to be fulfilled before some gift will be a real blessing. If the good thing came without our realising its source, the result might be to fix us in forgetfulness of God; and then it would have brought injury to us, not benefit.

934. PRAYER AND PHYSICAL OCCURRENCES
We still know very little about the control which spirit can exercise over matter, and the spiritual energy of fervent prayer may be a factor in determining some physical occurrences. God's view of the world is not like ours, along one line from past through present to an unknown future; it is eternal knowledge, and much which to us appears coincidence may be a connection planned by Him.

November Seventh

935. ETERNITY AND KNOWLEDGE

Even in human friendships there is the constant delight of new discoveries by each in the character of the other. Eternity cannot be too long for our finite spirits to advance in knowledge of the infinite God.

936. ETERNAL LIFE

If a man once knows the Spirit within him, the source of all his aspiration after holiness, as indeed the Spirit of Jesus Christ, and if he knows this Spirit of Jesus Christ within himself as none other than the Spirit of the Eternal and Almighty God, what more can he want? *This is the eternal life.*

937. ENTERING INTO LIFE

If we are to enter into the Life to which the Lord Jesus invites us, the self in us must be eliminated as a factor in the determination of conduct; if possible, let it be so effaced by love that it is forgotten; if that may not be, let it be offered. For if we are to *come to the Father*, self must be either offered or forgotten.

November Eighth

938. ORIGIN OF IDOL-WORSHIP

Merely to think things are one's duty or are good, without at the same time feeling them as good and obligatory, is not enough to control conduct. We have somehow to cross over from this, however accurate, yet shadowy and vague, conception of the Divine, into something which has compelling power. That is the reason why men make idols.

939. SELF-IMPOSED DISCIPLINES

The effort to crush self-concern by exaggerated austerities only leads to transference of concern from the self subjected to discipline to the self imposing it.

940. MORAL PRIORITIES

Few actions are guided by one motive alone, and the vital question in practice is not whether the motive of an action was noble or mean, but whether the just order of priority among motives has been maintained, so that when divergence arises the higher check and control the lower, and the lower do not control or check the higher.

November Ninth

941. EDUCATIONAL PURPOSE
We have learned a great deal about the technique of education. We have learned so much, indeed, of the technique of it, that we are in danger of forgetting the purpose of it.

942. DUAL SYSTEM
I would very daringly suggest that one value of the dual system is its duality. I wish to suggest that there is a very great advantage in the educational field in maintaining real variety of type, with a considerable measure of individual liberty and autonomy.

943. EDUCATIONAL DEFECT
Education is recognising as never before that its job is to develop personality, but refuses to guide its activities by any general conception of what personality is.

November Tenth

944. ART IS TIMELESS
In science it is true that the later supersedes the earlier; it is not true in art. Nobody supposes that, when perfect expression of some human emotion has once been given it will ever be thrown upon the scrapheap, because someone a hundred years later may do it again. He may do it again, but he will never do it better.

945. THE PRESENT
The present is so much of the empirical process as is immediately apprehended. This is far more than the passing sense-impression of the moment. It is all which is apprehended as continuous with that impression. And this may be an indefinitely long stretch of duration. A great work of art is always a unity, adequately appreciated only when grasped as a unity.

946. Worship and Kindliness

When we have been absorbed in great music, I do not think we generally feel particularly charitable to the people we meet outside. They seem to be of a coarser fibre than that into which we have been entering. That could never be true of our worship if it has really been worship of God, not some indulgence of our own spiritual emotion, but the concentration of mind, heart and will on Him. You will be full of kindness for everybody as you go out from such worship.

November Eleventh

947. Father

What was novel in the religious language of the Lord was His constant, His almost invariable, use of the word "Father" as the name of God.

948. "In the Name"

To act in the name of another is to act as His representative. When we pray in the Name of Christ, we pray as His representatives; in other words, we are then praying for what is already His will, but for a part of that will which He waits to fulfil until we recognise Him as the source of blessing by asking it of Him; then immediately His power is released and becomes effective.

949. Christ's Coming

The Coming is the Cross and the ingathering of its triumph through the Resurrection, Ascension, Pentecost, the Evangelisation of the World, and the final Consummation; its focal moment is the Cross and Resurrection.

November Twelfth

950. Facing the Material

The spiritual is not to be found by turning our backs upon the material and leaving it to go its own way. But the spiritual is above all to be found by facing the material in fellowship with God and using it to become the expression of the divine character as that reproduces itself in our own souls through the faith in us which it has itself evoked.

951. ESSENCE OF RELIGION
The heart of religion is acknowledgment by the finite of insignificance before the Infinite, by the sinner of pollution before the Holy, by the creature of total dependence before the Creator. It is in its essence a submission to authority.

952. LOCUS OF RELIGIOUS AUTHORITY
Thus a supposed contrast is drawn between religions of authority and religions of the spirit. But this is a false division. The less orthodox form is not independent of authority; it only finds its authority in a new place—in natural science, or in art, or in the momentary phase of literary fashion.

November Thirteenth

953. CHURCH WORK
The work of the Church is done, not by ecclesiastical officials nor under the direction of ecclesiastical committees, but by members of the Church who do the ordinary work of the world in the inspiration of Christian faith and in a spirit sustained by Christian prayer and worship.

954. COMMERCE
Commerce must become avowedly an exchange of goods for mutual advantage, in which all search for what is called a favourable trade balance is repudiated; the pursuit by every nation of a favourable trade balance is inevitably a source of conflict; for if the balance is favourable to one it must be unfavourable to another.

955. LOVE THROUGH JUSTICE
Is it not the fact that in problems concerning the relations of corporate groups of men, the way of love lies through justice?

November Fourteenth

956. CHOOSING A CAREER
What are you going to do with your lives? To choose your career for selfish reasons is a worse sin than, let us say, committing adultery, for it is the withdrawal of the greater part of your time and energy from the service of God. Of course you are not going

to be turned out of a club for doing it, but you will turn yourself
out of the fellowship of Christ by doing it.

957. Vocation in a Vicious Society
What a vicious social order sets us as our task can be performed
in the spirit of obedience to God, provided it be recognised that
a refusal to do it, as for instance in a strike against bad conditions,
may be made in the same spirit.

958. Vocational Service
It is very often true that our inclinations are a sure guide to our
vocation, for we like doing what we can do well; but the reason
why we ought to do it is that it will be of more use, not that we
shall like it better. Our motive in taking up an occupation should
be to serve.

November Fifteenth

959. Swiss Books
I have heard from a Continental scholar the suggestion that a
new international authority should require in all countries the
study of history from Swiss textbooks, which are very scholarly
and written from the point of view of an age-long neutrality. It
would be a good thing for all of us.

960. Educated Christian
What are the marks of an educated Christian? . . . I would say at
least three—knowledge, worship and grace: knowledge, the
apprehension in the mind of the verities of the Christian Faith;
worship, the approach in the heart to the God and Father of our
Lord Jesus Christ; and grace, the quality of life which results,
and makes the Christian man what he is.

961. Character-building
Should we prefer people if they responded mainly to the fear of
punishment or mainly to some bare conception of abstract duty?
Or do we prefer men who respond to the appeal of sympathy,
of love, and of devotion? If the latter, then remembering that the
appeal to any motive always strengthens that motive, we shall say

that this, and this alone, is the ground upon which character can be developed, and on which alone it is desirable that it should be developed.

November Sixteenth

962. CREDAL CONCEPTION OF GOD

What the Creed says of God is that He is the "maker of heaven and earth, and of all things visible and invisible"—anticipating all that science might discover and claiming it all for Him. . . . It is impossible to form a conception of God greater than that of the Creeds.

963. IDOLATRY

We have come falsely to suppose that the essence of Idolatry is found in the worship of material images; but that kind of idolatry comes second in the Decalogue. The first commandment is: "Thou shalt have none other gods but Me."

964. MENTAL PORRIDGE

What mental porridge, one wonders, will be the substitute for thought or conviction in those minds which have constituted themselves buckets to receive from the spout of the loud-speaker the skimmed-off cream of all knowledge and speculation current in our time!—From *Visitation Charge, 1936* (S.P.C.K.).

November Seventeenth

965. CALL OF THE CHURCH

We start from the misery of an aimless life in an apparently purposeless world, and from the desire to give allegiance to a leader and a cause and so gain significance for life. We offer as the cause to live for a truly universal fellowship and a Leader who appeals to all that is good in man or woman; and we show that He is actually fulfilling His promise in the world to-day.

966. DRAPED LANTERN

We may illustrate the nature of the Church as it exists now in the world by the figure of a draped lantern.

967. Church and Wealth

The Church, which is set in the world and has to carry on its activities through the instrumentality of worldly wealth, is under perpetual temptation to become attached to that wealth for its own sake; it is under obligation to resist that temptation; it does not follow that for the avoidance of the temptation it should abandon all wealth.

November Eighteenth

968. Religious Experience

By religious experience we ought to mean an experience which is religious through and through—an experiencing of all things in the light of the knowledge of God. It is this, and not any moment of illumination, of which we may say that it is self-authenticating; for in such an experience all things increasingly fit together in a single intelligible whole.

969. Legalism

If you make your religion into any form of code, so that it consists of regulations, two bad things are going to happen. You are going to frighten off the people who know they cannot keep your code. . . . It is bad for those who cannot keep the code; but it is much worse for those who can; for they get self-satisfied. In the parable of the Pharisee and the Publican the whole point is that the Pharisee was a much better man than the publican; only he was not going to become any better than he was that day unless something came to break up his self-complacency; whereas the publican was discontented and therefore might grow; with eternity before him he might come right home at last.

970. Uncharitable Christians

Insurgences even of noble aspiration are always perilous; they have a strong tendency to self-deception, and also to spiritual pride—the special sin of the devil. That is why very religious people are so often uncharitable.

November Nineteenth

971. NON-ANGLICAN PREACHERS

Until we have reached that consummation of union which will consist in full sacramental communion, it would seem to me wrong and false to admit as a preacher during the service of Holy Communion one who belongs to another communion than our own. On the other hand, to admit such a one to preach the sermon appended to Morning or Evening Prayer on the occasion of any enterprise of united witness seems to me appropriate and most desirable.

972. 1944 EDUCATION ACT

The real significance of the Education Act of 1944 is that it was born, not as all its predecessors were, in an atmosphere of bitter religious conflict, but in a spirit of partnership between the State, the education authorities, the teachers, the Church and the Churches.

973. CLERICAL DISQUALIFICATION IN SCHOOLS

It is utterly unjustifiable that a fully qualified teacher should be excluded from the State service on the sole ground that he also has the training and qualifications of another profession.

November Twentieth

974. CALAMITIES IN NATURE

We can make no plans and form no purposes unless we can count upon the regularity of natural process; and if this is the condition of all moral purposes, then, of course, there will be no longer any moral difficulty in facing those calamities which from time to time come upon mankind through this regularity of nature.

975. ACCIDENTS

It is good for us to be subject to accident. It is good for us to know that each one of us may quite easily be killed by motor-car or other engine of destruction. It is good for us to be under the constant reminder that "we have here no continuing city."

976. WONDER-WORKERS

He does not want the sort of excitement that miracles are liable to create. It is not fundamentally a spiritual interest; it is the interest in a wonder-worker, and we know how perpetually the Church is liable to fall under the spell of a wonder-worker.

November Twenty-first

977. CRITERION OF PROGRESS

The only unconditional criterion of progress is that supplied by the Christian Gospel: God is Love, so that progress consists in the increasing preponderance of goodwill and love over self-interest and ill-will.

978. SERVILITY

An attitude to life which expects and accepts benefits which have not been earned, whether in rich or in poor, is essentially servile in quality, and will lead to servility in the State however democratic its forms and machinery may be.

979. INFLUENCE OF GOVERNMENT

It is a fundamental principle of far-reaching importance that Governments affect the conduct of their subjects far more by the principles implicit in their acts than by the requirements of legislation or the severity of the penalties attached to neglect of those requirements.

November Twenty-second

980. SELF-EXAMINATION

Do not begin ever considering what is wrong with you without first being quite sure your mind is directed towards the glory of God as it has shone forth in Jesus Christ.

981. REPENTANCE AND AMENDMENT

Forgiveness is part of repentance; but there is all the difference in the world between coming to Him and saying, "I am sorry; I won't do it again; will you have me back?" and saying, "I think I can get rid, under the inspiration of the love You have shown, of all the little resentments and spites in my heart. May I come back?" It is the second that He requires; He says it over and over again; and He puts it in the prayer He taught us.

982. MORALITY MATTERS

There is nothing so insulting to a man as to pretend that his moral lapses do not matter. It is to treat him as below the moral level. And if we have reached that level at all, then nothing could be more dreadful for us than to suppose that God said, "Never mind." There is only one thing worse, I have heard it said, than to break your mother's heart, and that is to find out that she had no heart to be broken.

November Twenty-third

983. MONASTIC SYSTEM

With all its enormous virtues, the great objection to the monastic system appears to me to be this: it ignores the fact that you cannot cut yourself off from your generation and live in it a life which is altogether at variance with its principles. If you do, it will be something forced and not natural.

984. MOB RULE AND DEMOCRACY

The mere fact that a great number of people are united in the pursuit of an object is no sort of reason for supposing that it is a good object or that there is any merit in their union.

Sometimes it becomes important to dwell on that, especially at a moment when we are talking a great deal about democracy; because, of course, there has been a fearful lot of fustian talked about democracy: *vox populi vox dei:* what nonsense!

985. THE BEATEN WORLD

We do not have to conquer this evil world in any strength of ours; in spite of its brave showing, it is a beaten thing; and if we treat it so, in our own hearts or in the world outside, it will crack and crumple and dissolve.

November Twenty-fourth

986. AUTHORITY OF THE DIVINE CHARACTER

The spiritual authority of God is that which He exercises by displaying not His power, but His character. Holiness, not omnipotence, is the spring of His spiritual authority. In such a vision as that of Isaiah there is awe-inspiring majesty; but what leaps to the prophet's consciousness is not the sense of his power-lessness before the Almighty, but the sense of his uncleanness before the All-Holy.

987. GOD'S AUTHORITY
The spiritual authority of God Himself consists, not in His having the power to create and to destroy, but in His being the appropriate object of worship and love.

988. GOD: CREATOR AND REDEEMER
" 'Let there be light'; and there was light." "And He was parted from them about a stone's cast; and He kneeled down and prayed, saying, Father, if Thou be willing, remove this cup from Me; nevertheless not My will, but Thine be done. . . . And being in an agony He prayed more earnestly; and His sweat was, as it were, great drops of blood falling down upon the ground."
In those two quotations there is depicted the difference for God between creating the universe with all its millions of stars, and the making of a selfish soul into a loving one.

November Twenty-fifth

989. INTUITION
All value-judgments are in their nature intuitive, and they do not admit of argument. The faculty of intuition may be trained by practice, but in the moment of approval and disapproval there is no question of argument.

990. MORALS AND RELIGION
It may be true that our moral conceptions have been developed through that part of experience which is called religious, but it does not in the least follow that morality needs a religious basis to maintain itself.

991. THE MORAL JUDGMENT
The moral judgment, so far as I can understand it at all, is a value-judgment upon things and persons regarded as affecting society.

November Twenty-sixth

992. POLITICAL BIOGRAPHY

I happen to have a particular love for political biography which illustrates the interplay of private character and public events, which is at its height in political biography. I rejoice in such stories as that which Trevelyan gives us in one of the volumes on Garibaldi, about the way in which it was settled that Garibaldi should be allowed to cross the Straits from Sicily into Italy.

993. POETRY

I am in most sympathy with those whose interpretation of life is Christian, but I do not think that is the decisive feature. It does seem to me that the pure poetic form is better in the case of those who really have something to say, than in the case of those who are expressing distress because they have nothing to say.

994. IDEALS OF NOVEL-WRITING

I am disposed to say that among the worst books ever committed to paper is Hardy's great masterpiece, *Tess of the D'Urbervilles*, because to me it gives the impression that although Tess may no doubt be rightly described on the title page as a pure woman, the net result of the novel is to produce the impression that it does not matter whether she was or was not; and that is much more disastrous than if she had been, quite frankly, an impure woman. The creation of that sense of purposelessness and futility in life I regard as the greatest disservice any man can render to his fellows, whether through literature or anything else.

November Twenty-seventh

995. EACH AND ALL

Only the principle of divine love can give security that the welfare of each and the welfare of all is equally a matter of primary concern.

996. SOCIAL MOTIVES

We are bound to be concerned about housing, about nutrition, about social security, about freedom from unemployment and so forth; but let us be quite clear that our concern with every one of

234

these is dictated and directed by our primary principle—the development of persons in community as children in the family of God. That will cover very nearly every political proposal in the social and economic field.

997. A Shocking Evil
There are large proportions of our fellow citizens for whom the bottom is liable to fall out of life through no action of their own, but simply through the way in which our economic system is worked or works, and it is a shocking evil and we must fight against it.

November Twenty-eighth

998. Adoration
As the flower turns to the sun, or the dog to his master, so the soul turns to God.

999. Honour from God
Do I (I wonder) really care more about honour that God gives than honour that men give? Of course I know mentally that it is the more precious; but am I more eager to receive it?

1000. Free Acts for Love
We know that there is no action in life in which we feel so free as an action that we undertake in order to please a friend; yet the content of that action, the thing we do, is then determined by the pleasure of our friend; it is, so to speak, he who has really chosen what shall be done, and yet there is nothing that we do so freely.

November Twenty-ninth

1001. "Wanting" to do My Duty
If there are some people who say that, as far as they know, they do always want to do their duty as they see it, and nearly always want it even enough to do it, I may feel sceptical as to whether they are telling the truth, but in any case I should say, "That is their case, and not mine." Unquestionably, for such people Christianity has not got anything like so direct a value as it has for me.

1002. MOTIVE FOR SERVICE

If a man does in any degree whatever fear or love God and knows that the God whom he fears or loves cares intensely for all those other people who to him are either indifferent or repellent, then there is a new motive for serving them.

1003. SINS OF CLERGY

A besetting sin of all of us, who are concerned with the ordering of religious life and worship, is the loss of proportion and perspective, and the attribution of primary importance to secondary or even to tertiary and quaternary concerns.

November Thirtieth

1004. BREAKING RULES

We shall drift into futility unless we have rules; we rightly break our rules when we are convinced that we can serve God better by breaking them, but it must be because we are serving God better and not pleasing ourselves better.

1005. LEGALISM

Pharisaism had its roots in reverence and in loyal desire to obey God's will. But by converting occasional legislation and direction into a code for all times and places it corrupted the true character of the revelation in which it was grounded; and the same condemnation awaits all who follow the Pharisaic principle of seeking to order life by immutable rules.

1006. RELIGION AS "BUSINESS"

All "business" is a concern with means rather than ends; but religion is concerned with the supreme end of man. The clergyman who, because religion is his business, treats religion as a business, has sold the pass; yet it is very easy to slip imperceptibly into doing this. Yet the clergyman needs to be "business-like"; and if he fails in this, he is likely to damage his purely religious work.

DECEMBER

December First

1007. ACTING CHARITABLY

Unless we can be quite sure that our charity, whether it is towards poverty or towards sin, is not having the effect of saying, "Never mind," we shall be doing more harm than good; that is, we shall not really be acting charitably.

1008. REPEATING CHRIST'S ACTIONS

Until we ourselves have reached a far higher pitch of spiritual life than we have yet attained, it is not right for us to imitate the actions of Christ, because we shall not be producing the same effect as He produced. Our act after all is the whole train of circumstance which we initiate; so we shall not really be repeating the actions of Christ, because we shall not be bringing into existence the same result.

1009. RELIGION AND MORAL SENSE

The moral sense itself does not necessarily depend upon religion.

December Second

1010. GOODS OF THE SPIRIT

Material goods are limited in amount at any one time, so that it is true that the more one has, the less there is for other people. . . . But it is not true of the good things of the spirit, indeed of all those good things which we enjoy by our distinctively human faculties. It is not true of knowledge—that imparts itself; it is not true of the appreciation of beauty—that is infectious; it is not true of courage, which is more infectious still: it is not true of love and joy and peace—wherever these find a home they spread all round about it. And so when men put first the good things of the spirit they are always brought into fellowship, because here one man's success is everyone else's success.

1011. LEISURE AND UNEMPLOYMENT

The only difference between leisure and unemployment is whether you have some money to spend.

1012. THE SUPREME SPIRITUAL FACT
The actual fellowship of Christians of various ecclesiastical traditions and of almost all nations, including those at war with one another, is the supreme spiritual fact of our epoch.

December Third

1013. NATIONAL SELF-INTEREST
If there is to be any approach to a brotherly fellowship of nations before all men are converted to a life of perfect love, it must be by the method of so organising their relationship to one another that national self-interest will itself urge justice in action.

1014. CAPITALISM AND SOCIALISM
Our task must be to do justice as far as possible to the truth of capitalism, as well as to the truth of socialism.

1015. SEEDS OF TOTALITARIANISM
The modern Probation System started as the Police Court Mission of the Church of England Temperance Society. We are actually witnessing an extension of the concern of the State to include the whole welfare of Youth. In such developments we see at work the principle which, if allowed free play unchecked and unbalanced, produces the Totalitarian State.

December Fourth

1016. ATHEISTIC ENVIRONMENT
There was a time when in Christendom everyone picked up casually the Christian verities, whether or no he gave his mind to them. In most of what people pick up in the modern world, and indeed in most of what they give their minds to, there is a complete absence of Christian content, an implicit atheism.

1017. WORLD PEACE
The throne of the united world is not a Chair of State; its emblems are not sceptre, orb and sword; it is a Cross and the Crown is made of thorns. It is as worshippers at the Cross of Christ that we set ourselves to win for the world true peace.

1018. Effect of Secular Society

Secular environment is not yet Christian, and until it is, there is not the remotest chance of any individual person being completely Christian.

December Fifth

1019. A Baseless Dogma

God is at all times active in making delicate adjustments to varying circumstances, wherein the life of living personalities consists; in other words, we must challenge the scientific thinking of the world at its foundation and roundly deny its totally baseless dogma of uniformity.

1020. Constant Action

We shall not say that He has left nature as a closed system into which He periodically intervenes from outside, but rather that in all things He is active as a living person, directing His action according to the infinite wisdom that guides the fulfilment of the eternal purpose.

1021. The Focus of Doctrine

It is the faith of Christendom that in the Gospel there is given an unalterable revelation of the eternal God, not in the form of doctrinal propositions which once and for all have been drawn up for the acceptance of men of every age, but in the form of a Person and a human Life to which all the doctrinal formulations point us.

December Sixth

1022. "Use" of Forgiveness

Whether forgiveness is good for a wrong-doer or not entirely depends on how much it costs the person who forgives.

1023. Christian Citizenship

If we did all love God with all our hearts and our neighbours as ourselves, we should work our hardest to produce what the whole fellowship needed: we should take our own reasonable share of it and no more; and we should be eager that everybody else should have what he needed also, and there would be no need for property rights.

1024. COMPROMISE

We must compromise with the world on those points where we may be assisting the development of what is best in the actual circumstances of the society in which we live.

December Seventh

1025. INDIVIDUALISM OF SPIRITUAL WORLD

The whole harmony of creation depends upon the offering by each humblest spirit of its own appropriate note of music which no other can sound without discord. It is impossible to stress too strongly the individualism of the spiritual world; each is himself alone, and each, because an object of divine love, has infinite value.

1026. COMMUNISM OF SPIRITUAL WORLD

It is equally impossible to stress too strongly the communism of that world, if for once we may use the word "communism" with what ought to be its meaning; for each individual becomes his true self only so far as he fastens his attention not on his own fulfilment but on God and on God's work in creation.

1027. RELIGIOUS NEUTRALITY

We can hardly remain in an equipoise between belief and unbelief. We are inclining to one side or the other. As a wise man once said, "There's God and there's yourself; and you are settling down on one or the other."

December Eighth

1028. "DUTY" TO SELF

So far as I can see there can be no obligation to self. Obligation is the relation that exists between one conscious being and another, or perhaps it would be more accurate to say between one purposeful being and another.

1029. GROWTH OF MORALITY

The growth of morality is two-fold. It is partly a growth in content, from negative to positive. It is partly a growth in extent, from tribal to universal.

1030. CHRIST AND ETHICS

Our Lord brought ethics in its general principle to its final development, because beyond the love of all men you cannot go.

December Ninth

1031. FIRST CAUSE

When we have traced an occurrence to the Purpose of an intelligent being, we are satisfied. And this is natural enough, for in such a case Mind has referred the occurrence to itself as cause.

1032. MIND: ITS DISTINGUISHING FEATURE

Marx and Lenin, though insisting on the contrast between Dialectical and Mechanistic Materialism, and on the distinct reality of mind and its own processes, yet limit the activity of mind to reaction, according to those processes, to situations presented by the material order, so that mind is always secondary and dependent. We found on the contrary that the distinguishing feature of mind is its capacity for free ideas, and for directing its attention to those ideas apart from any material occasion for doing so.

1033. A FALLACY OF SCIENCE

It may be that in the practice of religion men have real evidence of the Being of God. If that is so, it is merely fallacious to refuse consideration of this evidence because no similar evidence is forthcoming from the study of physics, astronomy or biology.

December Tenth

1034. MY "NEIGHBOUR"

My "neighbour" is anyone with whom I have anything at all to do, even by accident, and even though he is the kind of person that I naturally hate or despise. I am to care as much for his interest and welfare as for my own; and I need a most penetrating "conversion" before I do that.

1035. "CHRISTIAN" ENGLAND

We live in a country where for many generations the Gospel and the faith which it calls forth have influenced the lives and thoughts of men. It is possible that even complete loyalty to Christ would not win its hatred; and certainly we must not suppose that in such a country ecclesiastical persons or assemblies are more sure to be true to the principles of Christ than are secular persons and assemblies discharging their proper responsibilities.

1036. THE BEST IN MAN

If you want to get the best out of a man, you must appeal to his loyalty, his affection, his devotion, his perception of what his conduct involves for others whom he cares for or who care for him.

December Eleventh

1037. SACRAMENTS AND ASSURANCE

It is by means of their formal correctness that Sacraments bring us the assurance which is independent of feeling; and it is by their materialism that they can represent and promise the complete control of the physical by the spiritual.

1038. LAY CELEBRATION

The objection to lay celebration is not that it is in its own nature inoperative, but that it is a usurpation by one member of what belongs to the whole Church. Strictly speaking, I submit, we should not say that a layman cannot celebrate, but that he has no right to celebrate, and it would therefore be wrong for him to do so.

1039. LAY ADMINISTRATION OF SACRAMENTS

Lay Baptism is only permitted in extreme emergency, and in the case of the Eucharist the emergency can only arise in the very rarest circumstances, for the individual believer can make a spiritual communion if there is no duly accredited minister to offer him sacramental communion, and in the strength of earlier communions can continue to feed upon Christ in his heart with thanksgiving.

December Twelfth

1040. SIN AND DUTY

I do not find that the recognition of a duty is of any great assistance to its performance. I am rather inclined, I think, to dislike a thing if it appeals to me simply in the name of duty; and if I understand St. Paul aright, so did he; "the strength of sin is the law," the prohibition of something which one wants to do merely makes one want to do it more than ever.

1041. THE "BAD" WILL

You may say that to know the right course ought to lead to following it; and if it does not, that shows that there is something the matter with us; yes, very well; but the fact that we are bad won't make us good.

1042. LOVE AND OBEDIENCE

If ye love Me, ye will keep My commandments; and if we don't, we shan't. Let no one deceive himself about that. There is no possibility of meeting His claim upon us, unless we truly love Him. So devotion is prior to obedience itself.

December Thirteenth

1043. ST. JOHN—AUTHORSHIP

The view which now seems to me to do fullest justice to the evidence is that the writer—the Evangelist—is John the Elder, who was an intimate disciple of John the Apostle; that he records the teaching of the Apostle with great fidelity; that the Apostle is the "Witness," to whom reference is sometimes made, and is also the "disciple whom Jesus loved."

1044. EPISTLES OF ST. JOHN

The Epistles are the work of John the Elder in every sense of the words. They exhibit a smaller vocabulary, and in some respects a more crystallised outlook and greater tendency to definition, than the Gospel of which the Elder is the writer but the Apostle is the true author.

1045. RECORD OF EVENT

When St. John records the words, "I will not leave you desolate; I come to you" (xiv. 16), their value is not only that this, or something fairly represented by this, was uttered, but that the thing described has happened.

December Fourteenth

1046. UNCHANGING PRINCIPLES

It is always true that the actual moral customs of a people depend on and are bound up with the social structure of their life; that is why different kinds of conduct are judged right or wrong in different parts of the world or at different times, while the principles of right and wrong remain unchanged.

1047. CONVENTIONAL BEHAVIOUR

Convention is not to be despised; it is the deposit of the experience of the community in which it is found, accumulated through many generations; but it depends upon the social context in which it arises. When that is greatly altered, especially if it is altered suddenly, whatever is conventional and no more will collapse.

1048. BETRAYAL OF A FRIEND

The religious life can make all the difference to morality, because to the religious man all his faults, which he will now call his sins, are no longer merely a breach of law; they are the betrayal of a friend. They were wrong before; and he knew it, but he did not mind. But the religious man must mind.

December Fifteenth

1049. RESPONSIBILITY

To shed responsibility is always to incur spiritual danger.

1050. SUNDAY ABUSES

One task that confronts us is to recover Sunday from the secular uses by which under the pressure of war it has been invaded, and especially to keep for young people on that day a fair opportunity to become educated Christians against the enticement of Sunday cinemas and the excursions of thoughtless parents.

1051. FINANCIERS AND BUSINESS MAGNATES

Our business mechanism and our financial mechanism are become so elaborate that those who work them are bound to give an immense amount of time and attention to the mere process of keeping them in order. And that makes it very hard to avoid falling into the error of making these things ends in themselves. They claim so much attention during life that it is very difficult to remember that, after all, their whole value lies in the service they can render to something beyond themselves.

December Sixteenth

1052. St. John and the Synoptists

A good photograph is vastly preferable to a bad portrait. But the great portrait painter may give a representation of a man which no photographer can emulate. And he does it by drawing what is not at any moment altogether actual. The Synoptists may give us something more like the perfect photograph; St. John gives us the more perfect portrait.

1053. St. John's Witness

We are not likely of ourselves to come closer to the Lord by exercising our coarse faculties upon the more exact record of words spoken and deeds done than by entering into communion of thought and feeling with the mind of that disciple who lay "breast to breast with God."

1054. The Beatitudes

It is to be noticed that in the Beatitudes, after the first, our Lord gives two series, one concerning the inward and one concerning the outward side; they are arranged alternately.

December Seventeenth

1055. Pain

Pain is in fact evil only in a secondary sense; it is something which, other things being equal, it is right to avoid. But it must always be chosen in preference to moral evil, such as treachery or cruelty; and when it is bravely borne, it has such an effect that we could not wish it away.

1056. Degrading Pain

It is harder to see the justification in the eyes of a righteous God of pain which degrades the sufferer, however guilty he may be, than of pain which ennobles the sufferer, however innocent he may be.

1057. Pain in God
Only a God in whose perfect Being pain has its place can win and hold our worship; for otherwise the creature would in fortitude surpass the Creator.

December Eighteenth

1058. A Christian Society
If our society is to be organised upon a Christian plan its whole tendency must be such as to suggest that the great aim of life is that it should be spent for the welfare of the whole; and this must apply as much to nations as to individuals.

1059. Christian Correction
What is the Christian method of correction? Not retributive, nor deterrent, nor even reformative punishment, but the conversion of the offender's heart and will by the readiness of his victim to suffer at his hands. That is the Christian method of meeting wrongdoing; it is absolutely central in the Christian creed.

1060. The Moral Law
The value of the moral law when reached does not depend upon the way in which it has been found.

December Nineteenth

1061. The Cross and Sin
It was not crime or vice that sent Christ to the Cross; it was respectability and religious stagnation and compromise.

1062. Change of Will
It is not that the Christian learns from Christ for the first time what the difference between good and evil is, but that his whole will is so changed that, as a matter of fact, he no longer wants to do the wrong thing.

1063. The Crucifixion
The Crucifixion was the worst thing that ever was done; and yet it was the best thing that ever happened. What the Chief Priests

and Pontius Pilate did was the worst thing that ever was done; but what God did in Jesus Christ was the very best.

December Twentieth

1064. THE POWER OF THE CROSS

The great Power which rules the world is submitting to suffer at our hands, in a way which can only be represented by the agony of Christ, and regards us as we inflict that agony in the way in which Christ regarded the people who sent Him to the Cross. . . . If we really feel that, it becomes intolerable. It is like finding that, without knowing what one did, one had struck one's mother in the face.

1065. THE CROSS AND OUR SIN

When one realises that the frame of mind that sent Christ to the Cross, alike in the Jews and in the Romans, is our own frame of mind to a very large extent, one has immediately a new horror of that frame of mind, and a new motive for wanting to be rid of it.

1066. HELL AS DOMINANT FEAR

The fear of Hell may check wrong tendencies, and so give the better side of our nature opportunity to grow; but as a dominant motive it can in the end do nothing but harm, because it is purely a selfish passion.

December Twenty-first

1067. "FINALITY" OF GOSPELS

The Gospel stories are not to be treated as something sacred, as a final authority, but as the means whereby we can come in touch with the living Christ who is the same yesterday, to-day and for ever.

1068. NO IMPOSED CONVICTION IN GOSPELS

It is the uncertainty about every *detail* of the Gospel record which finally secures its purely spiritual authority. Its general outline and its main facts—such as the Crucifixion—are assured. But if there were one detailed thing of which we could be absolutely sure and say there can be no doubt whatever that He did this or said that, no doubt of any kind, that would immediately be a binding fact, a hard nugget, so to speak, of imposed conviction which we should have to accept even though our spirits made no response to it.

1069. GROWTH OF CREEDS
The creeds are not objects of faith; they are expressions of a faith of which Christ is the object, and in regard to all such personal relationship there is scope for at least a great width of intellectual movement as we seek more and more perfectly to understand and to interpret the character with which we are confronted.

December Twenty-second

1070. BRIDE OF CHRIST
The Church is called the Bride of Christ when we think of it in its nature as the community that, having been redeemed, answers the love of Christ with responsive love.

1071. CHURCH AND SOCIAL ACTIVITIES
When the Christian principle has taken possession of men's minds sufficiently for the public authority of any nation or race to begin occupying this ground itself, it is probably wise that the Church should withdraw from a great deal of its activity and become rather the focus and source of inspiration, in the power of which the secular community undertakes activities which, without that Christian inspiration, would have been neglected.

1072. CHURCH AND PUBLIC LIFE
When the stage has been reached at which the public authority of any secular community accepts moral responsibility in relation to that community, the function of the Church becomes a proclamation of principles, the indication of features in the common-life which seem to involve denial of those principles and an insistence that those who are responsible should think out and undertake the necessary steps to make the principles apply.

December Twenty-third

1073. TRUTH, NOT MEDICINE

Our question is whether the Gospel of Jesus Christ, the Son of God, is true. . . . But we have got into the habit of thinking of religion as a kind of drug for the curing of the world's diseases. And so we ask whether the Gospel suits the African or the Arabian, the Indian, the Chinese, or the Japanese. . . . But if the Gospel is true, then the question is not whether it suits us, but whether we suit it. It is not the question whether it suits the Arabians, but whether they suit it; and so on.

1074. NUTRITIVE, BUT DIMINISHING

If you treat the Gospel as a drug, you go on and say: "Well, the diseases of the Western world are so-and-so and we think Christianity is the remedy for them; and the diseases of India are so-and-so and Hinduism is the remedy for them." But it would be rather odd, as a matter of fact, if the culture which produced the disease should also supply the remedy. It sounds like feeding the dog on its own tail; it is in one sense nutritive and in another rather diminishing.

1075. HAVING THE MIND OF GOD

The truth of things is what they are in the mind of God, and it is only when we act according to the mind of God that we are acting in accordance with the truth, in accordance with reality. Everything else is making a mistake.

December Twenty-fourth

1076. CHRISTIANITY, MOST MATERIALISTIC OF ALL RELIGIONS

It may safely be said that one ground for the hope of Christianity that it may make good its claim to be the true faith lies in the fact that it is the most avowedly materialist of all the great religions. . . . Its own most central saying is: "The Word was made flesh," where the last term was, no doubt, chosen because of its specially materialistic associations.

1077. THE CROSS AND BETHLEHEM

The shadow of the Cross falls over Bethlehem, and the world which crucified Christ was that world which could find no room for Him when He came.

1078. CHRISTIANITY: REVELATION RATHER THAN RELIGION

Remember that Christianity is not, first and foremost, a religion; it is first and foremost a revelation. It comes before us chiefly not with a declaration of feelings we are to cultivate, or thoughts we are to develop; it comes before us, first and foremost, with the announcement of what God is, as He is proved in what He has done.

December Twenty-fifth

1079. CHRISTIANS AND DAILY LIFE

There is always some danger that the very beauty of the Christmas story may lead us to let our keeping of Christmas be an interlude of joyful fancy inserted between the claims and cares of this harsh world. . . . Then it may no doubt bring joy while it lasts and some refreshment to weary spirits; but it will bring no inspiration or new strength; that can come only from what is as real as the duty to be done or the burden to be carried.

1080. GOSPEL SPLENDOUR

The overwhelming splendour of the Gospel of Christmas consists in precisely this—that the Lord of glory of His own will entered into our life of grief and suffering, and for love of men bore all and more than all that men may be called to bear.

1081. DIVINE DISCLOSURE

The Incarnation is not a condescension to our infirmities, so that "Truth embodied in a tale" may enter in at the "lowly door" of human minds. It is the only way in which divine truth can be expressed, not because of our infirmity but because of its own nature. What is personal can be expressed only in a person.

December Twenty-sixth

1082. REVELATION OF CHARACTER

It is always true that what gives occasion for the distinctions of personality to reveal themselves is something in the nature of an emergency, not the carrying on of the ordinary routine of life.

1083. What Loving God Is

If we think of some friend to whom we are especially attached we do not immediately think of what kind of presents he is likely to give us, but we are glad when we can be with him and we are glad when we can give him pleasure. That is what loving is. That is what loving God is.

1084. Supreme Honour of Ambassadors

God does not *need* our help; He could do quite well without us; but because of His love for us and for all men, He has made it the priceless reward of those who receive and obey His Gospel that they shall have the superlative honour of being His ambassadors.

December Twenty-seventh

1085. "Comparative Religions"

The "science of comparative religions." Might I implore you never to use that expression, even if some others do? There is no such thing as a comparative religion. You can't study it. There are a great many people who are comparatively religious, but it is not their beliefs and practice that are studied in this science. What it is, of course, is a "comparative study of religions." It is not a study of comparative religions, because there aren't any, and you can't study nothing at all, though a lot of students seem to spend their time at it.

1086. God and Actions

For the ancient Greeks, as for the Indian philosophies, God is an eternally perfect Being, existing unchangeably, so unchangeably as to be incapable of particular action. To put it crudely: He does everything in general, but He does nothing in particular.

We are perfectly familiar with this view . . . and against it . . . we must take an absolutely firm stand.

1087. Under Authority

"All authority has been given unto Me in heaven and on earth," the Lord is recorded to have said; "go ye, *therefore*, and preach the Gospel to all nations." "Therefore," because the authority is

His; because the only right and wise way for men to order life is under His authority.

December Twenty-eighth

1088. "HE WHO RUNS . . ."

Everything in its way will speak of God, and God will become to us, as He has been to the great saints, something more intimately real than any of these sights or sounds themselves, because each of them can hold the attention only for a moment whereas every one of them will speak of God.

1089. CHRISTIAN PROGRESS

As we become forgetful of ourselves and entirely filled with His glory, the glory of His righteousness and love, we become transformed into His image . . . from glory to glory; and because we are more like Him, we shall live more like Him; because we live more like Him, we shall do something that is far more truly His will than what we might have planned out for ourselves in an eager and perhaps impatient generosity.

1090. BEGINNING YOUR PRAYERS

Every time you come to pray you should first remember Jesus Christ, before you even offer praise, and certainly before you make any petition—and then, of course, make only such petitions as you believe He is ready to make in His heavenly intercession.

December Twenty-ninth

1091. PSYCHOLOGY AND KNOWLEDGE

The psychological student of religion very often fails to notice that he is avoiding the question whether the beliefs which he studies are true. . . . The student finds a belief concerning God and he draws out a scheme of the way in which this may have arisen in the mind of him who holds it. But that has nothing in the wide world to do with the question whether or not it is true.

1092. HISTORY OF BELIEFS

Why should the history of its growth be supposed to discredit a theological belief and not a psychological? If the history of an idea is all that can ever be said either in explanation or justification of it, that is as true of psychological as of theological theories.

1093. MEANING OF AUTHORITY

The proper meaning of authority is, of course, in its own nature an appeal to reason not in respect of the particular propositions commended by the authority, but in respect of the right of the authority to commend the propositions.

December Thirtieth

1094. BIBLICAL AUTHORITY

There has never been a devout person who in practice put the whole Bible upon one level or treated it as having equal spiritual authority. That is a dogma which has been erected on a purely theoretical basis with the very minimum of empirical foundation.

1095. OLD TESTAMENT CRITICISM

What modern study has done for us is not to remove the Old Testament from the position which it held for the first disciples, but, on the contrary, to restore to us, for whom it was not in the same sense a living tradition, that sympathetic attitude toward it which was natural at that time.

1096. HOLINESS IN OLD TESTAMENT

The first great illumination to be found in the Old Testament is the interpretation of holiness as first and foremost righteousness. What exalts God most completely in our mind is not that He is so great or that He is so powerful, but that He is so good.

December Thirty-first

1097. DESIGN

We, by the exercise of our own intelligence, are able to penetrate the secrets of nature, and always discover an order more exquisite in the perfection of each detail, more immense in the scope of its range, than our minds can begin to compass. We cannot any longer hesitate in supposing that behind the world of nature there is at work a power, guided by principles such as those which appear also in our own minds.

1098. ORIGIN OF MORAL JUDGMENT

Where does the moral sense come from? Of course, you will hear it said by many that it comes from the history of the society in which we live. Yes, the whole if its content does, but not the power of moral judgment itself.

1099. RELIGIOUS FAITH

Religious faith does not consist in supposing that there is a God; it consists in personal trust in God rising to personal fellowship with God.

INDICES

Index of Subjects

259

263

Penalties, 513, 560, 673, 674, 679, 789, 862
Penitence, 288
Pension, 823
Perjury, 890
Personality, 80, 82, 85, 226, 359, 370, 534
  distinctions in, 1082
  sanctity of, 73, 74, 530
Persuasion, 423
Peter, St., 510
Petitionary prayer. *See* Prayer.
Pharisaism, 183, 900, 969, 1005
Philanthropist, 392
Philosophy, 400
Planning and freedom, 625
Plato, 234, 535
Poetry, 112, 880, 993
Politics, 457, 533, 535, 586, 605, 606, 607, 680. *See* State.
  Christians in, 623, 624
Porridge, 964
Poverty, 254
Prayer, a, 787
  and daily work, 134, 377, 474
  answer to, 273, 752
  auto-suggestion and, 544
  beginning, 932, 1090
  Book language, 695
  consultation, 786
  essence of, 18, 379
  faith in, 111
  for enemies, 754
  futile, 140
  Lord's, 654, 785
  mediated, 543, 753
  perseverance in, 478
  petitionary, 16, 141, 467, 475, 542, 948
  self-forgetfulness in, 109, 476
  selfish, 272, 477, 653
  strength, 637
  thanking, 477
  unanswered, 17
  use of words, 110
Preachers, non-Anglican, 971
Preaching, 407, 409, 449, 650, 651
Predestination, 154, 419, 420
Present, the, 945
Pride, 566, 591, 600. *See* Self-centredness.
Principle of explanation, 26
Principles, Christ's, 213, 235
  moral, 1046
Probation system, 1012
Problems, human, 215, 239, 263

Procreation, 521
Production, object of, 40
Profit motive, 42, 494, 495, 584, 680, 681, 806, 881
Progress, 63, 66, 173, 305, 320, 431, 455, 562, 564, 565, 576, 738, 977, 1089
Promise, keeping a, 85
Proof, 700
Property, 39, 145, 765
Prophecy, locus of, 204
Prophets, 117, 203, 428
Prophylactics, 523
Protestantism, 429
Psychology and knowledge, 25, 125, 1091, 1093
  and logic, 278
Public control, 682
  opinion, 315, 555, 901
Punishment, 251, 865, 1059
Purgatory, 333
Purpose, constancy of, 669
  intelligent, 26

QUARRELS, 697

RAILWAY TICKET, 804
Reality, 31, 90, 369, 483, 484
Real Presence. *See* Eucharist.
Reason. *See* Intellect.
  and authority, 389
  and guidance, 139
Redemption. *See* Cross.
  cost of, 65, 66, 159, 296, 297, 298, 444, 648, 705, 741, 864, 989
Reformers, 428, 430, 431
Reformation, 717
Reincarnation, 250
Relativity, logical, 35, 124
Religion and intellect, 447
  and miracles, 883
  bad, 249, 440
  comparative, 1084
  departmental, 151, 152
  distinctive moments in, 930
  essence of, 951
  needing, 386
  neutrality, 817
  tradition and, 811
  union of all, 929
  using, 501
Religiosity, 735, 736
Religious experience, 197, 968
Repentance, 181, 445, 749, 854, 855, 981

266

Key to Book References

BC. *Basic Convictions*. Hamish Hamilton.

C. *Citizen and Churchman*. Eyre and Spottiswoode.

CC. *A Challenge to the Church* (Presidential Address to National Society, June, 1945). National Society.

CHC. *Christ in His Church*. Macmillan.

CLF. *The Church Looks Forward*. Macmillan.

COM. *Christianity and Communism*. S.P.C.K.

CTT. *The Church and Its Teaching To-day*. Macmillan.

EPC. *Essays in Christian Politics and Citizenship*. Longmans.

F. *Christian Faith and Life*. S.C.M. Press.

FN. *Foundations*. Macmillan.

H. *The Hope of a New World*. Macmillan.

J1. *Reading in St. John's Gospel* (1st Series). Macmillan.

J2. *Readings in St. John's Gospel* (2nd Series). Macmillan.

K. *The Kingdom of God*. Macmillan.

L. *Resources and Influences of English Literature*. National Book League.

MC. *Mens Creatrix*. Macmillan.

N. *Nature, Man and God*. Macmillan.

NP. *Nature of Personality*. Macmillan.

P. *The Preacher's Theme To-day*. S.P.C.K.

T. *Thoughts on Some Problems of the Day*. Macmillan.

YQ. *York Quarterly* (January, 1939).

Index to References

148. N309	204. N342	260. N470
149. J1.88	205. N323	261. J1.147
150. J1.91	206. F27	262. J1.197
151. T26	207. P58	263. J1.91
152. T26	208. N481	264. H14
153. T27	209. P56	265. T202
154. N501	210. F79	266. H64
155. N472	211. P55	267. P52
156. N511	212. N43	268. F48
157. N391	213. P65	269. N195
158. N471	214. N479	270. F84
159. F80	215. C44	271. N416
160. N461	216. N352	272. F114
161. N463	217. J1.68	273. F120
162. N480	218. C74	274. F35
163. J1.56	219. J1.199	275. J1.99
164. F81	220. J1.56	276. T163
165. N416	221. F74	277. T164
166. N464	222. F87	278. N33
167. N185	223. J1.107	279. N496
168. N186	224. H28	280. N13
169. N468	225. P26	281. F94
170. N501	226. C.O.M. 14	282. F101
171. N399	227. H49	283. J1.49
172. N351	228. F27	284. T124
173. F28	229. L8	285. J1.98
174. F43	230. N324	286. T126
175. F43	231. N448	287. C43
176. N217	232. N481	288. P46
177. N467	233. C29	289. F100
178. N504	234. J1.196	290. J1.118
179. H123	235. H91	291. F128
180. H123	236. T38	292. C54
181. F71	237. H56	293. N484
182. J1.15	238. H102	294. T106
183. J1.142	239. J1.62	295. N485
184. J1.140	240. F97	296. N401
185. F37	241. J1.109	297. N414
186. N515	242. N446	298. N397
187. J1.125	243. N315	299. N277
188. N216	244. N268	300. N490
189. N199	245. N410	301. N330
190. N228	246. F137	302. C55
191. N517	247. F18	303. N183
192. F132	248. N436	304. N.P. 42
193. N334	249. N22	305. J1.121
194. T118	250. N477	306. T6
195. J1.81	251. N455	307. P71
196. T120	252. N424	308. H24
197. H30	253. N421	309. P55
198. N194	254. C66	310. N469
199. J1.133	255. J1.163	311. N192
200. C21	256. C77	312. N191
201. N349	257. T10	313. F52
202. H99	258. C.O.M. 12	314. N190
203. N341	259. T200	315. F66

820. CLF176	876. J2.210	932. F110
821. CLF167	877. J2.210	933. H31
822. CLF168	878. L14	934. H33
823. CLF138	879. L14	935. J2.310
824. F61	880. L20	936. J2.310
825. N354	881. CLF109	937. J2.410
826. P79	882. CLF110	938. F23
827. J2.295	883. K124	939. N375
828. J2.xiii	884. F60	940. N374
829. J2.xxiv	885. J1.184	941. CLF48
830. T115	886. F65	942. CLF52
831. C59	887. J2.386	943. CLF81
832. C100	888. J2.387	944. F28
833. C42	889. J2.271	945. N203
834. C41	890. T50	946. F19
835. T90	891. T56	947. J2.231
836. N449	892. T63	948. J2.236
837. T35	893. CLF80	949. J2.294
838. C97	894. CLF84	950. P44
839. K112	895. CLF84	951. N343
840. K119	896. J1.85	952. N333
841. K67	897. P59	953. C48
842. N179	898. J1.71	954. H43
843. T26	899. CLF40	955. C78
844. F64	900. BC62	956. F36
845. J2.288	901. F66	957. H114
846. K91	902. F65	958. F32
847. K93	903. N513	959. CLF171
848. N57	904. C92	960. CC2
849. N489	905. CLF2	961. K128
850. N227	906. CLF2	962. T199
851. CLF110	907. K99	963. N22
852. CLF128	908. CLF154	964. —.
853. CLF132	909. CLF120	965. H116
854. F78	910. CLF148	966. C57
855. N173	911. CLF24	967. C66
856. P55	912. CLF4	968. T25
857. CLF148	913. K99	969. F95
858. CLF148	914. N511	970. T27
859. CLF150	915. H120	971. CLF10
860. H94	916. N358	972. CC8
861. C6	917. —	973. CC9
862. C30	918. —	974. BC20
863. K81	919. N459	975. BC21
864. K82	920. CLF173	976. BC39
865. K97	921. F26	977. CLF40
866. N145	922. P62	978. CLF41
867. N313	923. J2.xxvii	979. CLF67
868. F80	924. J2.xxviii	980. F69
869. H115	925. J2.xxxi	981. F85
870. C98	926. T90	982. P58
871. C57	927. C67	983. K84
872. T159	928. YQ476	984. CLF142
873. T119	929. K103	985. CLF96
874. T147	930. K104	986. N348
875. J2.267	931. J2.215	987. N349

988. F73
989. K43
990. K42
991. K47
992. L19
993. L23
994. L16
995. CLF133
996. CLF135
997. CLF121
998. N487
999. J1.203
1000. P56
1001. K61
1002. K62
1003. J2.349
1004. F101
1005. N343
1006. C72
1007. K85
1008. K86
1009. K53
1010. CLF108
1011. CLF109
1012. CLF179
1013. H92
1014. H52
1015. C33
1016. CC3
1017. CLF184
1018. K73
1019. CTT45
1020. CTT46
1021. CTT35
1022. K86
1023. CLF145
1024. K95

1025. N425
1026. N425
1027. J1.50
1028. K48
1029. K48
1030. K52
1031. N220
1032. N498
1033. N11
1034. J2.223
1035. J2.271
1036. K98
1037. T125
1038. T110
1039. T111
1040. K59
1041. K60
1042. J2.238
1043. J2.x
1044. J2.xi
1045. J2.xvii
1046. CLF73
1047. CLF73
1048. K64
1049. CC5
1050. CC5
1051. CLF144
1052. J2.xvi
1053. J2.xvi
1054. K122
1055. J2.257
1056. J2.257
1057. J2.385
1058. K77
1059. K80
1060. K52
1061. K65
1062. K66

1063. CLF101
1064. K63
1065. K62
1066. K129
1067. BC46
1068. BC47
1069. P31
1070. CTT19
1071. CTT19
1072. CTT20
1073. BC80
1074. BC81
1075. BC78
1076. N478
1077. BC54
1078. F34
1079. CLF93
1080. CLF94
1081. J2.231
1082. P15
1083. BC37
1084. BC92
1085. BC79
1086. BC20
1087. BC78
1088. BC22
1089. BC29
1090. BC75
1091. CTT31
1092. CTT31
1093. CTT26
1094. BC32
1095. BC33
1096. BC18
1097. BC12
1098. BC14
1099. BC16